LIVING YOGA

*52 Weeks of Inspiration to
Center and Enhance
Everyday Life*

13-Digit ISBN: 978-1-64643-028-4
10-Digit ISBN: 1-64643-028-X

This book may be ordered by mail from the publisher. Please include $5.99 for postage and handling.
Please support your local bookseller first!

Books published by Cider Mill Press Book Publishers are available at special discounts for bulk
purchases in the United States by corporations, institutions, and other organizations.
For more information, please contact the publisher.

Cider Mill Press Book Publishers
"Where Good Books Are Ready for Press"
PO Box 454
12 Spring Street
Kennebunkport, Maine 04046
Visit us online! www.cidermillpress.com

Typography: Agenda, Amatic, Eplica, and Gotham
All images used under official license from Shutterstock.com

Printed in the USA
2 3 4 5 6 7 8 9 0

LIVING YOGA

*52 Weeks of Inspiration to
Center and Enhance
Everyday Life*

RACHEL SCOTT

CIDER MILL
PRESS

BOOK
PUBLISHERS
KENNEBUNKPORT, MAINE

CONTENTS

Introduction 7

A (Very) Brief History of Yoga 13

52 Contemplations 27

Conclusion 197

Poses 201

Index 221

INTRODUCTION

I STARTED PRACTICING YOGA more than 20 years ago for the physical benefits. My hamstrings loosened up, my back felt better, and I became physically stronger. After practicing for a few years, I began noticing other, more powerful emotional and mental shifts: I felt less anxious, more grounded, and more self-aware.

While the physical practice helped me to become stronger and more flexible, the more profound impact of yoga was how it benefited my mental health. As I learned more about the Yoga tradition, I realized that the tools that had been helping me to practice on the mat were now powerful resources for living life off the mat. My yoga practice was becoming a lifelong ally that could support me in navigating life and relationships with more grace, integrity, and compassion.

For thousands of years, yogis have been interested in how we connect to our essential nature and live our best lives. *Living Yoga* is an opportunity to explore the richness of the Yoga tradition and apply these ancient tools and practices to help you live your best life.

HOW TO USE THIS BOOK

In this book, we will draw from the vast and varied history of yoga to explore concepts, key ideas, and practical tools that support us to navigate our modern lives with more grace and joy. Together, we will explore how yoga's ancient ideas can help us gain a clearer recognition of who we are, as well as help us to lead more vibrant lives. Yoga is not just about asana practice; in this book, you will experience how the rich philosophical depths of yoga can support your life and well-being off the mat.

There are several ways to enjoy this book:

▶ I have compiled 52 contemplations; you may wish to read one contemplation per week, and use the week to explore how these ideas and concepts resonate in your daily life.

▶ You could read the book from start to finish in any time frame you wish.

▶ The contemplations are indexed by topic. When you find that you are feeling stuck or curious, select a topic that resonates with you and let the book guide your journey.

Some weeks will simply include reflections for contemplation; other weeks may include suggestions for practices to help you navigate the ideas presented. Yoga is, after all, a practical tradition, and part of its richness lies in the tools that it offers.

Ultimately, the yoga path is personal: as you explore, notice what supports you to feel healthy and whole.

A yoga teacher, mentor, and educator, **Rachel Scott** helps teachers and studios around the world to create teacher trainings and continuing education programs. Her extensive knowledge and experience include earning two masters degrees, authoring three books, and leading over 4,000 hours of teacher training. As a writer and speaker, she continually wrestles with the juicy bits of life: relationships, authenticity, and discovering meaning in this crazy, wonderful world. She holds an E-RYT 500, YACEP, BA, MFA, and MSci and is a wicked coffee drinker. Learn more at rachelyoga.com.

TIPS FOR PRACTICES

Meditation is often offered as a tool for insight. Here are a few practical suggestions for your practice:

▶ Setting a timer may help you create a specific time frame for your meditations. I suggest starting with five minutes, and adding time as you like.

▶ When preparing to sit for meditation, take time to make yourself comfortable and find a position that helps you maintain a tall spine. If you're comfortable on the floor, it can be helpful to sit on a cushion, block, or blanket to reduce tension in your hips and create space for your spine to stay lifted. You may also find it supportive to sit against a wall or in a chair. If sitting is not comfortable, then feel free to lie down in a supine position.

▶ Sitting for a length of time can sometimes get chilly. If you tend to get cold, put on warm socks or grab a blanket in order to stay comfortable.

Some styles of meditation urge practitioners to sit with discomfort. However, I am more a fan of honoring your body's needs. Freely move to adjust your position if you feel any discomfort or pain. Although you want to avoid moving for the sake of distraction, prioritize your self-care and honor your body in all practices.

A (VERY)
BRIEF HISTORY
OF YOGA

FOR THOUSANDS OF YEARS, yogis have been asking, "Who am I?" and "How can I be happier?" For most of its history, yoga has not been an exploration of physical practice, but rather a deep and devotional inquiry into the depths of human consciousness.

Yogis have wrestled with such questions as:

► Who am I?

► What is my purpose?

► What is my mind?

► What is my soul?

► Is God separate from this world?

► What is suffering?

► How can I experience a life of liberation and freedom?

Yoga philosophy is part of one of the oldest continuous cultures on the planet: Hinduism. Hinduism is an umbrella for the wide array of schools and philosophical ideologies that evolved in India over the last several thousand years. Like a great tree, Hinduism has many branches. However, although many of the philosophical schools of thought have different practices or ideologies, they are all oriented to two central questions:

"Who am I?"

"How can I be liberated from suffering?"

Yoga is one of the branches on this tree.

Throughout its history, Indian culture has tended toward inclusion rather than suppression. Competing philosophical schools were more prone to debate than domination. This attitude allowed divergent schools of thought to flourish and evolve over time. The different philosophical schools of Hinduism called *darshanas*, or "viewpoints," and their variety demonstrate how each philosophy can provide a different way of looking at the same thing.

"The Blind Men and Elephant" story is a metaphor for this outlook. According to the tale, village inhabitants had never seen an elephant before. When an elephant arrived in their village, they ran to their local wise men, all of whom were blind.

Each blind man felt a different part of the elephant.

One felt a tusk and said, "Ah, it's like a rhino!"

One felt the tail and said, "It's like a horse!"

One felt its sides and said, "It's a great wall!"

One felt its trunk and said, "It's a snake!"

> "There are hundreds of ways to kneel and kiss the ground."
> —Rumi

The wise men were in complete disagreement about what the elephant really was because they each only had one part of the story. From a different perspective, however, each wise man was sharing the truth. Although their perceptions were different, they each were expressing an aspect of the truth.

Applying this story to the philosophical schools of Hinduism, we can see that no point of view would discredit another; each simply has a different access point to the truth.

There are six "orthodox" schools of Hinduism that trace their origins back to the Vedas (the oldest Hindu texts):

- Samkhya
- Yoga
- Nyaya (logic)
- Vaisheshika (atomism)
- Mimamsa (interpretation of the Vedas)
- Vedanta ("end" of the Vedas)

There are also three philosophical schools that do not cite the Vedas as their scriptural authority and are categorized as "unorthodox":

- Buddhism
- Jainism
- Carvaka

Like siblings, these different philosophical schools have grown up and played with one another, exchanging ideas like sisters might trade clothing. However, unlike the other schools, Yoga tends to focus on practice—rather than theoretical understanding—as a means to liberation and insight.

The umbrella of Yoga covers a wide array of different philosophies and practices. If the Yoga tradition is one branch on the tree of Hinduism, it is a branch with many offshoots and variations.

The origins of Hinduism are shrouded in mystery, but many scholars trace its roots back more than 4,000 years to the Indus Valley Civilization. The Indus Valley Civilization emerged in northwest India and Pakistan, where several ancient cities sprung up along the Indus and Sarasvati Rivers.

The earliest texts of Hinduism were composed during this time. The Vedas, from the root word *vid*, which means, "to know," are the first sacred Sanskrit texts. The Vedas are considered *shruti*, or "revealed wisdom," which means that they were created by humans, but were channeled from a higher source through divine insight. The Vedas include a variety of texts, including ritualistic chants delivered by priests. These early rituals were likely shamanic in tone, and used sacrificial fires and precise recitations to appease the gods and ensure that the natural and social order ran smoothly.

One of the last additions to the Vedas was a group of texts called the Upanishads. The Upanishads are also considered shruti, and are revelatory stories and contemplations emerging from the ecstatic (and perhaps intoxicated) state of its practitioners. These contemplations are metaphysical in nature and look deeply into the nature of self and identity. The Upanishads emerged from the meditations of groups of ascetics who fled society to retreat into the forest and focus on their personal liberation. You can almost envision these practitioners as ancient hippies who left society in order to pursue countercultural spiritual practices.

Upanishad means "sit down near," likely reflecting the close relationship between the guru (teacher) and student. Interestingly, although the earlier chants of the Vedic priests were used to uphold natural law and order, the writings of the Upanishads are intimate in nature. These meditating ascetics were far more interested in personal spiritual liberation than in upholding social norms. although the Upanishads are in one sense an extension of the philosophical insights of the Vedas, they also mark a radical departure in thought. The external rituals that characterized the Vedas became internal rituals of self-mastery. Rather than offering fire sacrifices to the gods, the ascetics instead sacrificed their attachments to ego, society, and worldly pleasures to experience divine insight.

The Upanishads gave birth to many of the core concepts that formed the foundation of Yoga philosophy, including the prana (energy), karma (the residue of cause and effect), the role of the guru, and the practice of meditation as the path to enlightenment.

The wisdom of meditative insight became crystallized in The Yoga Sutras of Patanjali, composed around 200 CE. This text is a series of short aphorisms that details the workings of the mind and outline practical tools that support the pathway to yoga, or liberation. This text illuminates the complexity of the mind's workings and provides practical tools to support practitioners on their spiritual journeys. As in the Upanishads, practitioners were advised to leave the distractions of society and avoid all sensual pleasures (including relationships, meat, and alcohol) in order to achieve liberation. Living a spiritual life required fasting, abstinence, and worldly renunciation.

Fortunately, for those of us who aren't interested in living in remote caves, Yoga philosophy evolved to include "householders" (people with family, living in society). The Bhagavad Gita, composed more than 2,000 years ago, made yoga accessible to everyone by offering new paths for practice that did not require worldly renunciation. A thousand years later, tantric philosophy revolutionized the practice, declaring that the world (and therefore the human body) was the expression of divine consciousness. With this new perspective, the material world was no longer an obstacle to spiritual liberation, but a living expression of divine consciousness. This world-positive viewpoint opened the door to a range of new tools that leveraged the sensory world as a pathway to spiritual liberation, including subtle body practices, sound, and mantra.

From the bosom of tantra, hatha yoga emerged as a philosophy that expanded the use of body-centered practices (including breath practices, cleansing techniques, and *asana*) as tools for practice and liberation. Several hundred years and a trip across the ocean later, and we now find ourselves practicing yoga postures and breath control as a means to control the mind, reduce stress, and increase our general well-being.

TEXTUAL REFERENCES

For our philosophical concepts, we will primarily refer to two different texts from the Yoga tradition: *The Yoga Sutras of Patanjali* and the Bhagavad Gita.

Composed around two thousand years ago, these texts contain many of the essential ideas that inform the Yoga tradition and our practice today.

The Yoga Sutra was compiled around 200 CE. Although authorship is attributed to a sage named Patanjali, this may be a *nom de plume* for different contributors. The name Patanjali literally means, "fallen offering," suggesting that this text was received from heaven as a gift. Sutra means, "thread." The book is a series of short, concise "threads" that could be memorized by students. Each thread encapsulates ideas and wisdom that could be the further subject of discussion and interpretation. *The Yoga Sutra* summarizes the key insights of the *jnana* (wisdom) Yoga tradition, which used meditation as its primary tool for spiritual liberation.

Patanjali's worldview was dualist. In a dualist philosophy, the spiritual world and the material (physical) world are considered separate. In order to achieve liberation from suffering, the practitioner sought to escape the physical world and connect instead to the spiritual world. Practically speaking, this

For ease of communication, I will frequently refer to Yoga "texts." However, until the Middle Ages, most ideas and scriptures were memorized and transmitted orally rather than written down.

means that practitioners would renounce society, disregard the impulses of their bodies, and pursue and internally direct experience. Although this worldview may seem impractical (or even distasteful) to those of us who enjoy relationships, sensual delights, and the good company of others, *The Yoga Sutras* offers many profound insights on the nature of the mind and the human condition that remain universally relevant.

The Bhagavad Gita, translated as "The Lord's Song," is part of a vast epic called *The Mahabharata*, or "Great War." This sweeping story contains highly entertaining and dramatic tales of conflict, gods, romance, and magical creatures. In the Bhagavad Gita, we encounter Arjuna, a warrior on the brink of engaging in battle with the opposing side of his family. Although his cause for war is just, Arjuna is wracked with doubt and indecision as he considers the violence that will ensue.

Arjuna represents us. In our daily lives, we are also are often caught between a "rock and a hard place," where we don't know what to do. The Bhagavad Gita explores the essential conundrum: How can I be a yogi, when I sometimes have to do hurtful things? Is it possible to be a yogi and still participate in the world? The Bhagavad Gita provides an alternative to the traditionally ascetic practices of yoga, that promote renouncing society.

Fortunately, Arjuna has a trusted adviser on his side. Krishna is a god who appears as Arjuna's charioteer. Krishna represents the voice of our highest self, and inner wisdom. When Arjuna implores Krishna for help, Krishna reveals three yogic paths that will allow Arjuna to do his duty, or dharma, and uphold his spiritual integrity. These three paths are *jnana yoga*, *karma yoga*, and *bhakti yoga*, or the yoga of wisdom, action, and devotion, respectively. The Bhagavad Gita is a handbook for "living your yoga," and empowers practitioners to navigate the conflicts and drama of daily life with compassion, wisdom, and integrity.

Zen in its essence is the art of seeing into the nature of one's own being, and it points the way from bondage to freedom. By making us drink right from the fountain of life, it liberates us from all the yokes under which we finite beings are usually suffering in this world.

—D. T. Suzuki

52
CONTEMPLATIONS

1. WHO AM I?

Yogas Chitta Vritti Nirodhah

Since the dawn of consciousness, humans have been wrestling with the questions, Who am I? and How can I be happier?

For yogis, the answer begins with a fundamental mistake: we believe that we are what we think. In other words, we believe that thoughts such as I am a good person, I am a failure, I am a great mom, or I'm sad reflect our core identity. Let's look at this more closely.

The human mind is a spectacular engine of invention. Our capacity to connect disparate objects and ideas has spawned the invention of our greatest innovations, from early discoveries like metals, tools, and the wheel to more recent ones that have allowed us to traverse the continents, create global communication, and travel to the moon.

Although the mind is humankind's most powerful and precious tool, it comes with a dark side. The same power that propels innovation can also drive us to anxiety, depression, doubt, and despair. When we follow our thoughts into imagined shadow realities, we can become overwhelmed by negativity or fear.

To make it worse, we conflate our sense of self with this constantly changing and tumultuous landscape. When we think, I am good or I am bad we attach that label to our core identity. We assume that our sense of self is defined by what we think, feel, or do. When we think, I am a good worker, I am an accountant, I am a failure, or I am a success we believe that these labels define our core identify. But these labels are always changing.

> "There is nothing either good or bad but thinking makes it so."
>
> —William Shakespeare, from *Hamlet*

When I was younger, I moved from New York City to Vancouver, Canada, to embark upon a new life adventure with my fiancé. Before this great change, I had a comfortable and secure sense of self that was anchored to several identifiers: New Yorker, actor, loving girlfriend, American, strong woman.

Fast-forward a year: everything had fallen apart. My marriage had cracked open when my husband started drinking. I lived in a foreign country surrounded by strangers, and my career had disappeared. Suddenly, all of the happy identifiers I had previously enjoyed had been destroyed. My new labels were awful: expatriate, failed wife, obscure actor, enabler.

When we attach our sense of self with our changing and subjective experience, we set ourselves up for a wild roller-coaster ride of self-esteem.

Thousands of years ago, the yogis observed that our minds are always changing. Rather than attaching our sense of self to the constantly changing opinion of our minds, yogis offer a different point of view. They suggest attaching your sense of self to the part of you that is unwavering and consistent. This aspect of self is called *purusha*, which could be translated as your "soul," "higher consciousness," "presence," or "witness."

A Yoga text that was composed nearly 2,000 years ago, *The Yoga Sutras of Patanjali*, summarizes this understanding. The first few sutras capture the heart of the text. Loosely translated, they are:

- "Yoga is the restraint of the fluctuations of the mind stuff."
- "Then the seer (the self/witness/soul/consciousness) abides in (perceives) its own nature."
- "At other times, the Self appears to be the mind stuff."

In other words, when our minds are still, we perceive who we really are. When our minds aren't still, we mistake the content of our minds (the "mind stuff," like our thoughts and feelings) for our true selves.

Imagine that you are sitting by a lake. When the wind blows across the lake, the surface of the water is distorted. However, when the lake is calm, then the water can reflect the spaciousness of the sky. In the same way, when our minds (the lake) are disturbed by thoughts (the wind), then our true nature is obscured. But when our minds (the lake) are calm, they can reflect our true self or soul (the sky).

According to *The Yoga Sutras*, we are not our fluctuating thoughts or feelings; we are the presence, or purusha, that witnesses and observes our experiences. When we identify with purusha, rather than the content of our minds, we are in a state of yoga. When we are not present, our sense of self is misguidedly attached to our ever-changing thoughts and feelings.

Identifying with our minds can be called, "the great mistake." It is a classic case of mistaken identity in which we attach our sense of self to the wrong thing.

The yogis call this fundamental misperception *avidya*, which is Sanskrit for "non-seeing."

Thank goodness, it is surprisingly simple to correct this mistake.

By pausing and watching our thoughts, we can create space to question our habitual narratives. Simply put, we can choose to not believe everything we think. We can *watch* the story, rather than *be* the story.

One of my teachers explains this fundamental insight through the following story:

Imagine you are in a movie theater. You sit in your seat, the lights go down, and the movie comes on. Soon, you are so engrossed in the story that you forget you are watching a movie. When something exciting happens on the screen, you feel excitement. When something tragic happens, you feel sad. When there is happiness, you feel elated. When something scary happens, you feel afraid. But even though you are experiencing an emotional joyride, you have been safe in your movie seat the entire time.

We are like that moviegoer. We are immersed in the stories, emotions, relationships, and drama of a movie called, *My Life in A Human Body*. But while we may get caught up in the story, we are in reality quite safe as the unchanging witness watching the show.

When we can be less attached to the content of our stories — and more connected to the space of the witness — we can enjoy the wild ride of life without getting so frustrated by its changing and uncertain nature.

PRACTICE

▶ Take a comfortable seat.

▶ Close your eyes.

▶ Take a few deep, clearing breaths.

▶ Begin to notice your thoughts as they arise.

▶ Rather than follow your thoughts, instead allow yourself to watch them as they come and go.

▶ Enjoy the space between your thoughts.

▶ Sit in the seat of the watcher.

REFLECTION

▶ Throughout your day, pause to notice your thoughts. Are they true? What if they are not true?

▶ Who are you — your thoughts or the watcher?

2. LETTING GO OF BAGGAGE

Karma Yoga

Do you ever feel stuck in your stories, or in the "baggage" you carry with you from a previous experience?

For example, say that you were chased by a dog as a child. The outcome of that scary experience may be a fear of dogs, even though another dog may be quite friendly. If you have had your heart broken, you may become afraid of vulnerability and intimacy. Negative experiences usually create a reactive fear so that we avoid repeating the event. However, not all baggage is negative: a daily meditation practice may create a helpful mental routine for managing stress.

As a personal example, I was raised as a "nice" girl. I was taught to be polite, avoid conflict, and only speak when I had something nice to say. Although this training gave me a healthy respect for others' points of view, it also left me woefully ill equipped to wrestle with the interpersonal conflicts of my first marriage when my husband with alcoholism decided to start drinking again. To navigate my marriage, I had to recognize and question my habitual "nice girl" conditioning.

Ultimately, all of our experiences—good, bad, and ugly—leave an imprint that colors our perceptions of the world around us. According to the concept of karma, everything we do, think, feel, and say leaves an impression, or *samskara*. These imprints continue to accumulate throughout our lives, shaping the way we perceive and act. According to ancient yogis, the cycle of karma was a problem, as it doomed us to reincarnate into a continual cycle of suffering, or *samsara*. After all, if you keep creating karma when you're alive, then you'll just have to keep coming back to the world until you work it out. From a modern point of view, we might think of samskaras and karma as the habituation of neurological pathways. Neurons that "fire together, wire together." The more we practice certain behaviors or habits, the more conditioned we will become to repeat those same actions.

Although some of our habits may be useful (for example, a daily meditation practice that reduces stress), some may undermine our well-being (like a daily three-martini lunch). Changing our conditioning, particularly when it's become deeply engrained, requires the intention and willpower to change.

How can we navigate living a full, rich life and avoid the pitfalls of accumulating additional karma? The Bhagavad Gita provides a path. Composed around 500 BCE, the Bhagavad Gita was part of a great epic story called *The Mahabharata*. In this fantastical tale, the warrior Arjuna is given counsel by a god, Krishna.

Karma: cycle of cause and effect; residue of the cycle of cause and effect

Samskara: impression, imprint

Samsara: the cycle of life and suffering

Arjuna is in a bind similar to ours: How can we take action—particularly if it's going to create more conflict and karma—and also be a yogi? After all, living in the real world requires interacting with other people and taking action, which naturally leads to karma and conditioning. So how can we be free?

Krishna outlined a revolutionary new type of yoga called karma yoga, or the yoga of action. According to Krishna, it is impossible to avoid action. As human beings living on the planet, we must breathe, eat, drink, walk, talk, and engage with the world. We cannot help but take action. Rather than avoid worldly interaction, Krishna suggested that attitude is everything. When we engage in action and are selfishly attached to the outcome, then we will create more karma. However, if we do our best in the moment and then surrender to the results of the actions, we can continue to be in the world karma free.

Consider this: How much of your thinking is caught up in what you did, what you should have done, what you could do, or your planning? Our mind's tendency to dwell on and rehash past regrets and future intentions keeps us from being fully in the present moment. But, if we could relinquish our attachment to outcomes, then we would be able to be more awake moment to moment.

Karma yoga invites us to be fully alive in the present moment by letting go of our relentless (and futile) attempts to control everything around us. Karma yoga asks us to be mindful of what we can actually control (our actions, right there and right now) and what we cannot (everything else).

> "Yoga is skill in action."
> —Bhagavad Gita

For example, I spent many years believing I was responsible for other people's reactions and feelings. Because of this mistaken viewpoint, I would bend over backward to avoid conflict, remain likeable, and keep the peace—which didn't always work. (If I actually had control over anyone else's feelings, I would be delighted to wave a wand and make everyone happy!)

By becoming clear about our own scope of responsibility, we are better able to take meaningful action, while recognizing the limits of our power.

REFLECTION

▶ How much of your thinking is devoted to replaying the past or imagining the future?

▶ What are you taking responsibility for now that is beyond your control?

▶ In what parts of your life can you take true responsibility for your own actions and agency?

▶ How does being in the present moment help you to make better choices?

3. LETTING GO OF FALSE IDENTITIES

Neti, Neti.

What makes you, you? Your clothes? Your job? Your body? The external trappings of your life can change. You can change clothes, jobs, your marital status, and where you live. But does this change who you really are?

Or, consider physical changes. Perhaps you dye your hair, grow older, sustain an injury, gain or lose weight, or change your gender. Do any of these changes alter who you really are?

To find what is eternal and unchanging, consider an ancient thought experiment called *neti, neti,* or "not this, not this." This exercise asks you to discard everything that is impermanent by saying, "I am not this." When you have discarded everything that you are not, you are left with (the perhaps indescribable) experience of what you are.

....

"Only to the extent that we expose ourselves over and over to annihilation can that which is indestructible in us be found."

—*When Things Fall Apart,* Pema Chodron

....

PRACTICE

Find a comfortable, easy seat. In this meditation, you will take time to consider some of the different elements in your life one by one. Consider if each element is a component of your core, unchanging identity. If it is not, then discard it by thinking, Not this.

Once you have completed a list of neti, neti, sit in the space of what remains.

Here are some examples of elements you might examine:

- ▶ I am not my clothes.
- ▶ I am not my family's behaviors.
- ▶ I am not my job.
- ▶ I am not my family.
- ▶ I am not my identity as a mother.
- ▶ I am not my face.
- ▶ I am not my weight.
- ▶ I am not my relationship.
- ▶ I am not my thoughts.
- ▶ I am not my feelings.
- ▶ I am not my anger.
- ▶ I am not my fear.
- ▶ I am not my ego.
- ▶ I am not my mistakes.
- ▶ I am not my addictions.
- ▶ I am not my habits.

REFLECTION

- When you find yourself feeling anxious or stressed, ask yourself, Where am I vesting my sense of self? What is false that I am protecting?

- In my confusion, what do I believe is *me* that is not me?

- Is the essential *me* — my true self — really at risk?

- When I pause, and take several deep breaths, is there really anything wrong in the present moment?

4. CONNECTING TO THE ABSOLUTE

Om

The word *om* is as old as the first Hindu texts, the Vedas, where it is used as an emphatic exclamation. By the time of *The Yoga Sutras*, Om was understood to represent *Isvara*, or "pure awareness." You can translate the term *Isvara* with a term that is personally resonant for you, such as universal consciousness, the absolute, the Lord, or cosmic intelligence.

In *The Yoga Sutras*, sutra 1.27–1.28, Patanjali reveals that Isvara is represented by the sound *om*, and that through the practice of repeating *om*, its essence may become clear.

In these sutras, Patanjali offers a potent and accessible tool for connecting to our highest selves: we can simply repeat the word *om*, and through this repetition, we will begin to naturally resonate with universal consciousness. In Yoga philosophy, Sanskrit words are not simply representations of objects; the sounds themselves embody the essence of what they describe. The repetition of words can therefore be extremely powerful.

Chanting *om* is like striking a tuning fork, in which we attune ourselves to a higher vibration. Not coincidentally, the sound of *om* is very similar to another sacred word, amen. The sound of both of these words invites us to resonate with something that is greater than ourselves.

The practice of Zen is forgetting the self in the act of uniting with something.

—Koun Yamada

PRACTICE

▶ Find a comfortable seat so that your spine is tall and easy.

▶ Take a few deep, slow breaths and focus on the sensations of your body.

▶ Quietly and slowly, repeat the mantra *om*, allowing yourself to sense the vibration of the sound.

▶ Repeat it 10 to 15 times.

▶ Rather than chanting *om* out loud, chant *om* silently to yourself about 10 times.

▶ Feel the internal vibration of the sound.

▶ Let the mantra go, and take a few deep breaths.

▶ Notice any shifts in your state of being.

5. CHANGING NEGATIVE THOUGHTS

Pratipaksha Bhavanam

We can be very hard on ourselves. The self-talk in our minds is often negative, critical, and driven by worry. When we start to believe in the spinning stories in our head, we can begin a spiral into anxiety or sadness.

In the *Yoga Sutras* 2.33, Patanjali says, "*Vitarka badhane pratipaksha bhavanam*," which Swami Satchidananda translated as, "When disturbed by negative thoughts, opposite [positive] ones should be thought of."

How simple! How practical! And what a relief to recognize that humans have been struggling with bad thoughts for thousands of years.

Although the goal of yoga is ultimately to realize that we are presence (the inner witness, soul, or consciousness; in Sanskrit, *purusha*), it's useful to become friendly with our minds. Until we reach enlightenment and transcend our minds, we might as well cultivate a thought garden that is lush and nourishing rather than destructive. At the very least, considering ideas that challenge our mind's habitual judgments and criticisms will help create the space to recognize that the mind is subjective.

The judgment of the mind is often protective in nature. Over time, we have developed an "inner critic" voice to proactively protect us from failure, hurt, or vulnerability. However, left untended or unchallenged, we can start to believe the judgments in our heads are an accurate view of reality, rather than simply a protective mechanism.

Part of our personal growth is the practice of pausing so that we can question our conditioning, reevaluate our preexisting narratives, and see our situation from a more informed and compassionate perspective.

PRACTICE

Write out all the judgments that come into your mind. It may be useful to try this exercise for several days to keep a record of the many criticisms that arise and to notice any particular repetitions. The simple act of acknowledging and recording the voice of your inner critic will help you to create room from identifying with it.

For example, my own inner critic comments include:

▶ You're not fit.

▶ You're fat.

▶ You're not successful enough.

▶ You're lazy.

▶ You don't try hard enough.

▶ You're a crappy daughter.

▶ You're selfish.

For each judgment, write down a truthful antidote. If you have a hard time dislodging a criticism, then imagine the voice of an inner friend or cheerleader who can exuberantly defend you against these judgments.

Be energetic, enthusiastic, and unapologetic in your statements. The inner critic is an irrational tyrant who does not listen to reason; sometimes you just have to shout her down.

For my list, I might choose the following phrases as antidotes:

- ▶ I make healthy choices.
- ▶ I am beautiful at any size.
- ▶ I am successful.
- ▶ I work really hard.
- ▶ I am a loving and devoted daughter.
- ▶ Go away! (Or something stronger.)

Once you've written your antidotes, say them slowly and emphatically out loud in a strong, clear, and grounded voice.

Write out your favorite antidotes and post them somewhere that you can see them, or tuck them into your wallet.

REFLECTIONS

▶ Begin each day with a positive affirmation of your selfhood.

▶ Notice when the mind starts to travel on a familiar negative train, and use the emphatic statements of your "inner friend" to devalue and dismiss these judgments.

6. HOW TO RELATE TO HAPPY PEOPLE

Have you ever encountered someone who was happy...and it drove you crazy?

Although we may hope that we would be happy when someone else is joyful, sometimes that's not how it goes. Do any of these situations resonate with you?

▶ You've just entered a raffle for a free trip somewhere wonderful that you really, really, really want to win. But your friend wins the trip instead. You offer her congratulations, but are secretly jealous and sad that you didn't get the prize.

▶ You've been trying to get pregnant, but are having issues. Your friend shares the news that she is expecting. You want to be happy for her, but feel devastated.

▶ You have been struggling in your relationship. Your friend has just fallen madly in love and is waxing ecstatic about the wonder of romance. You roll your eyes and think, Yeah, just wait till it gets *real*.

▶ You're strapped for cash and have been working hard to make ends meet. Your sibling gets a promotion that comes with a spectacular raise.

If we aren't doing so well, or if someone seems to have something we want, then it can be challenging to feel friendly in the face of their happiness. Their happiness might seem to highlight our own sense of wanting.

For example, when I was an actress, competition for paying jobs was fierce. Often my friends and I would audition for the same role. Many times, they landed the job, and I didn't. Though I put on a cheerful face, my internal reaction to their good news was somewhere between self-flagellating despondency and bone-biting jealousy.

If I dug a little deeper, my reaction was a symptom of a much deeper problem: I was outsourcing the responsibility for my self-esteem to someone else. Rather than find a sense of wholeness and worthiness in myself, I was expecting that something outside of me—in this case, a job—would make me feel good about myself. In the acting business, I was usually giving a casting director—a perfect stranger—the keys to my self-esteem kingdom.

My self-criticism and sadness came from the misguided belief that my sense of worthiness depended on my professional success. Ironically, even if I *were* successful at an audition, my initial rush of confidence would dissipate with the next botched audition. I lacked stability in my own sense of self-worth.

Negatively reacting to another's happiness is usually a symptom of the great mistake. The great mistake occurs when we affix our sense of self and our worthiness to something outside of us. The material world, or *prakriti*, is constantly changing. After all, even mountains crumble eventually. When we rely on the external world—jobs, possessions, appearance, or reputation—to provide us with reassurance, we will ultimately be disappointed.

The yogis suggest that your true self, or purusha, is not subject to change, but is steady and eternal. You can connect to self by simply pausing, letting go of attachments to your thoughts, and connecting instead with the deep presence that is within you.

When you encounter happiness in others, practice (and it may indeed at first be a practice!) cultivating friendliness toward them and their situation. If you have negative feelings, trace them back to the root cause, and create space to connect to your own presence.

The more we practice cultivating friendliness toward those who are happy, the deeper our own sense of resilience, wholeness, and abundance will grow.

REFLECTION

▶ When have you struggled to delight in someone else's happiness?

▶ What lack in yourself were you imagining?

▶ Proactively practice cheerleading another in their happiness.

▶ Cultivate a small daily practice that helps you calm your mind and connect to the space of your presence.

7. HOW TO RELATE TO SAD PEOPLE

When someone is sad, how do you react?

▶ An acquaintance is devastated over an old breakup that was clearly for the best. Though you appreciate that she's sad, her moping is starting to get irritating.

▶ Your friend made a bundle on a hot stock tip, then lost it all. Though he's sad about the loss, you secretly feel relieved that you're not in his shoes.

▶ A former co-worker left your workplace with high hopes of branching out on her own. You'd always wanted to do the same, but were worried about the risk. When her business is struggling, you feel smug that you made the right choice.

Although we all wish we would react with a kind ear, sad people can bring impatience, frustration, discomfort, or even enjoyment to the surface.

Patanjali understood the human mind, and he knew that the majority of our internal drama can be triggered by other people. In sutra 1.33, he offers some practical advice for relating to others so that we have the best chance of retaining our equanimity — rather than being triggered and reactive. He advises that we cultivate *compassion* toward the unhappy. Interestingly, Patanjali is not recommending that we are compassionate because it will make us a good or moral person, but because compassion helps us to most easily retain our own peace of mind.

When we have an adverse reaction to someone's unhappiness, it is a sign that the other person's situation has triggered an attachment within us. Perhaps we feel uncomfortable because we relate too closely to their situation, or we might feel relieved that we have escaped their unfortunate fate. When we do not react with compassion, it's a sign to dig deeper in ourselves and notice what is really going on.

One of my friends was involved in a very intense relationship with her girlfriend. They would continually break up, then get back together, only to break up again. My friend was often perpetually sad that they couldn't resolve their differences and would bemoan their relationship's on-and-off-again status. Rather than feeling compassion for her, I instead felt irritated and frustrated. I wanted to give her a good smack on the side of the head and say, "Snap out of it, already!"

Digging a little deeper into my reaction, I realized that I felt triggered because my friend was repeating the exact same behavior I had exhibited in a previous relationship of my own. Her situation reminded me all too clearly of how confused and sad I had felt in similar circumstances and I didn't like being reminded of my behavior.

Cultivating a true attitude of compassion toward the unhappy is not simply about putting on a sympathetic face and saying the right words. The real work is to recognize when there is an obstacle to our natural empathy, and to root out what has triggered our reaction. In this way, we can clear away the obstacles to our own goodwill, so that our compassion may flow easily and naturally. From an authentic open heart, we can then hold space that is genuine, loving, and supportive for others.

REFLECTION

▶ Notice when you feel an obstacle to compassion. Where is the obstacle coming from?

▶ Sometimes we have trouble feeling compassion for ourselves when *we* are unhappy. When do you struggle with self-compassion? What are you judging about yourself?

▶ How can you support yourself to develop authentic compassion for your own sadness or grief?

8. HOW TO RELATE TO VIRTUOUS PEOPLE

Have you ever seen a movie that involved police corruption? Usually, there's a cop on the take who is trying to convince his new and idealistic partner that it's okay to accept "protection money." The new partner resists crossing the line, much to the consternation and anger of the corrupt officer. Drama ensues!

In this movie plot, the corrupt police officer is not very happy with the "virtuosity" of his partner.

Perhaps you can relate to some of these other ways that we may react to people who are virtuous:

▶ Your friend raves about her new green-smoothie health food kick, and you've just chowed down your second doughnut. Rather than congratulating your friend on her virtuousness, you poke despondently at your belly and lament your lack of discipline.

▶ You desperately need to vent about your irritating coworker, and your friend gently reminds you that she doesn't like to participate in gossip. You feel irritated that she is so judgmental.

▶ You're finally out for a fun night on the town, and suggest that everyone gets a second round of drinks. Your friend passes, saying that she wants to stay clearheaded and doesn't like to drink too much. You feel deflated and annoyed.

According to sutra 1.33, Patanjali advises us to "delight in the virtuous."

A virtuous person could be described as someone who is upholding the elevation of their own values at the expense of personal comfort. Upholding values could include donating time to a good cause, making healthy food choices, or using money conscientiously. On a grander scale, upholding one's values could involve standing up to tyranny or exposing corruption at personal expense.

Although it seems that we should naturally admire the virtuous, virtuosity can be irritating when it exposes our own *lack* of virtuosity.

For example, let's say that you are out with a friend, and you want to order dessert. "Want to split something?" you say, hoping your companion will indulge with you. She demurs, "No, I'm avoiding sugar these days." You may feel disappointed and even irritated that your friend won't get off her high horse and have a little fun.

In this moment, your friend's refusal to join you in dessert exposes your own internal conflict. If you felt 100 percent okay about eating dessert, you would cheerfully order the double chocolate fudge cake. Instead, her refusal sparks your own internal conflict between the sensual enjoyment of eating something delicious, and supporting the longevity of your own health. If she had joined you in dessert, you could have swept your internal conflict under the rug. But her refusal puts you in the uncomfortable position of having to consciously acknowledge your own choice.

When we don't experience an instinctive "delight" in the virtuous, it's a sign that we are experiencing an internal conflict between what we want to do—and what we believe we *should* do. Our values are in conflict, and we don't like the way it feels. In response, we may feel defensive, exposed, or defiant.

From an objective point of view, virtuous actions should instill admiration. After all, the world is a better place when humans are willing to be uncomfortable in order to do the right thing.

When someone else's virtuosity triggers us it is a sign that we need to do some internal work on our own values. We can either buck up and practice doing the "hard thing," or we can practice self-acceptance and embrace that we are the kind of person that occasionally just loves to eat cake. In either scenario, the responsibility for self-consciousness is ours.

REFLECTION

▶ As you move through your day, notice the choices that you are making. What values are you upholding?

▶ When you are indecisive, which values are in conflict?

▶ Consider someone you admire. Which values are they upholding that you wish to develop in yourself?

9. HOW TO RELATE TO WICKED PEOPLE

Swami Satchidananda translates sutra 1.33 as: "By cultivating attitudes of friendliness toward the happy, compassion for the unhappy, delight in the virtuous, and disregard toward the wicked, the mind-stuff retains its undisturbed calmness."

Consider the following scenarios:

▶ Your coworker is clearly slacking on work and not pulling his own weight, and it's driving you crazy! Every time you see him getting coffee or chatting on the phone, you want to throw your laptop at him.

▶ You see a bully on a playground, picking on a smaller kid, and want to give her a dose of her own medicine.

▶ The news is running story after story about large companies that are cheating on regulations and dumping illegal pollutants into the oceans. You feel despair.

How do we respond when faced with wickedness? When we cannot change the situation, disregarding the wicked can be useful for our own peace of mind.

For example:

▶ You refrain from getting into a futile debate with someone you consider to have damaging political views.

▶ You have no control to change a situation or something bad that has happened in the past.

If you are interested in justice, then Patanjali's advice to "disregard" the wicked may seem like a hard pill to swallow. Patanjali wasn't interested in saving the world or punishing the unjust; his priority was to help you retain the calmness of your mind.

However, although we want to avoid ruminating over someone else's wickedness, this does not mean that we cannot take action to rectify a wrong. In sutra 1.33, Patanjali advises you to have "compassion for the unhappy" and to "delight in the virtuous."

When you see a bully picking on someone at the playground, "disregarding the wicked" may not be as important as having "compassion for the unhappy" or "delighting in the virtue" of fairness. Out of compassion for the bully's victim, you may choose to take action.

Whether or not we act, Patanjali would advise us to notice the state of our mind. Are we able to let the remembrance of these wicked acts go, or do we continue to give them a life of their own within our heads?

In one story, an old monk and a young monk walk down to the river. A beautiful woman is trapped on this side of the river. The old monk carries her across the river and she goes on her way. After a couple more miles of walking, the younger monk finally bursts out, "We have taken a vow of celibacy. How could you carry that woman across the river?" The old monk looks surprised and says, "My dear boy, I left her there. Why are you still carrying her?"

REFLECTION

When you feel upset by someone else's unscrupulous acts, consider:

▶ Do you have the power to change circumstances for the better?

▶ Will taking action ease the rumination of your mind?

▶ If not, what do you gain by continuing to hold on to it?

10. WHY AM I HERE?

Dharma

Many yoga traditions would propose that your goal in this incarnation is to recover your connection with your truest nature, and to yoke your identification to your true self. Through the practice of yoga and meditation, you can begin the process of self-realization, and recognize that your core identity is not attached to your thoughts and feelings, but is uncovered when you connect to your internal witness, or presence. You experience yoga (union) when you are properly connected to this deep awareness that lies within.

This is the soul's purpose, to remember its personal and eternal connection to the divine. From a yogic perspective, you don't have to work to create the connection; it's who you fundamentally are. The work is to remove the obstacles that stand in the way of this realization.

Although remembering our intrinsic divinity is certainly nice, we may also be interested in worldly work. According to the Bhagavad Gita, our dharma or duty, is our worldly purpose. We are instructed that it is better to do our own dharma, no matter how humble, than to do someone else's, no matter how exalted.

It is important to ask "What does life want of me?" We are usually consumed with trying to get something from

Tat tvam asi: thou art that. You are what you are seeking.

life; how refreshing and what a relief to think instead of what we are here to provide!

Sometimes we can become afraid if we don't connect to a grand purpose in our life. I should know what my purpose is or what I need to do, we may worry. Instead, ask, "What is this present moment asking of me?" Start moment to moment. This moment may be asking you to read this book, rest your body, be a compassionate ear for a friend, earn a living, support your children, or take care of your body. Each moment will bring an opportunity to explore your own purpose—and how you can live your yoga.

> "Ultimately, man should not ask what the meaning of his life is, but rather must recognize that it is he who is asked. In a word, each man is questioned by life; and he can only answer to life by *answering for* his own life; to life he can only respond by being responsible."
>
> —Viktor E. Frankl, *Man's Search for Meaning*

Your dharma can change over the course of your life. At one point you may be dedicated to your studentship, and at another time it may be your highest value to be good mother. By revisiting What does life want from me?, we can stay open to fresh impulses and information.

As another point of view, according to bhakti yoga (yoga of devotion), the greatest purpose we have is to love. Every act is performed as an expression of devotion and reverence. No matter what worldly work we undertake, we can give our actions meaning by infusing them with our love. When in doubt, add love to your actions and you will never go wrong.

REFLECTION

▶ What is asking from me?

▶ In the past, have I had moments in which I have been clear on my purpose? What gave me that feeling of clarity?

▶ Beneath the mind's voices of fear, criticism, or judgment, is there something that my soul is calling me to do?

▶ What types of activities bring me joy?

Happiness is when
what you think, what
you say, and what you
do are in harmony.

— Mahatma Gandhi

11. INTENSITY

Tapas

Throughout yoga history, fire has been used for purification and transformation. In the time of the Vedas, priests performed ritual sacrifices and used smoke to send sacrifices to the gods. Later, yogis engaged in austerities (purification practices) such as fasting and abstinence, and used the "fire" of their discipline to harness their minds. During the time of *The Yoga Sutras*, Patanjali named fire as an essential component of a yogi's practice. Today, we use the intensity of the physical practice to make our bodies stronger and help focus our minds.

Tapas literally means "heat," and can be translated as, "the willingness to endure intensity for the sake of transformation." Yogis recognized that change involves discomfort; we need some fire to hold to a new course of action rather than slide into the comfort of a familiar habit.

Humans are wired to seek the path of least resistance. However, the path of least resistance often won't get us what we really want. To our goals—be they worldly or spiritual—we need some grit. Intensity can take many forms, and arises most often when we are confronted with a challenge or change. Staying present when comfortable routines are tested requires fortitude.

For example, I can feel a good deal of intensity if I wake up in the morning and find out that I'm out of coffee, challenging my creature comforts. I also experience the heat of tapas when my yoga teacher asks me to hold plank pose longer than I may like. Though I may start to shake, I can recognize the value in confronting my own perceived limitations. Psychologically, I experienced a great deal of personal intensity when my engrained identify as a "nice girl" who avoided conflict began to shift. I had to learn to unravel years of conditioning to find a voice and speak up for myself in a healthy way.

It's important to note that tapas is intensity *for the sake of transformation*. We aren't engaging in discomfort pointlessly, or simply to develop power. We challenge ourselves because we wish to uphold a higher value beyond our personal comfort. By mindfully engaging in tapas, we can generate the necessary fire to clear old habits, make changes, and consciously manifest our will in the world.

REFLECTION

Recall a time of great intensity:

▶ How did intensity serve you?

▶ What did you learn?

▶ Would the learning have been possible without the intensity?

As you encounter intensity, ask:

▶ Is this intensity for a higher purpose?

▶ What value am I upholding by challenging myself?

12. SEXUALITY

Brahmacharya

For much of its history, Yoga philosophy advised practitioners to be celibate. After all, because the goal of yoga is to create equanimity in the mind, it made sense to advocate practices that avoided riling us up. You only have to think back to your big first crush to remember how much sexual attraction can create a thought tornado! To avoid this tumult, yogis practiced *brahmacharya*, or abstinence. After all, if temptation is off the table, then the mind may have a better chance of staying calm.

Early yogis were not impressed with the world or their bodies in general. They believed that the material/ physical world (prakriti) and the spiritual world (purusha) were separate. Connecting to one's spiritual nature meant focusing on their internal experiences and avoiding distractions of the body, including pleasure, food, alcohol, and sex.

With the emergence of tantric philosophy around the sixth century, a more positive attitude toward the world—and body—emerged. According to tantric philosophy, the material world is the unfolding expression of universal consciousness.

Let's explore what that means.

First, what is universal consciousness? Universal consciousness is divine intelligence and awareness. You might also call it God, soul, collective consciousness, cosmos, or universal love. The tantric yogis called it *shiva*. At an individual level, it's known as purusha.

On the other hand, there is the energy of manifestation called *shakti*. Ultimately, shakti is responsible for the expression of prakriti, which is composed of the five elements, or *mahabhutas*: earth, air, water, fire, ether. Everything in the physical world is subject to the *gunas*, or forces of nature. Unlike the steadiness of shiva, shakti is in constant flux. Everything that is part of shakti has a cycle: arising, sustaining, dissolving, then arising again. In tantric philosophy, shakti and shiva are two sides of the same coin. If you think of a candle, shakti is the flame, and shiva is the light. You can't have one without the other.

Here is another way to think of it from the point of view of physics:

If you imagine the universe before the big bang, all of space, time, energy, consciousness, and matter was condensed into one impossible singularity. This singularity is expressive of the fundamental unity of shiva-shakti. Once the big bang occurred, this singularity expanded into a multiplicity of elements, including space, time, and matter. The consciousness and intelligence of the universe would be shiva, but the matter and energy within it are shakti. However, traced back to their source—and from the highest perspective—they are one.

So, what does all this mean for sexuality?

Before tantra, the material world—shakti—was generally regarded as an impediment to the spiritual practice. Ascetic yogis would avoid the sensual pleasures of the world entirely and focus exclusively on their connection with the spiritual. However, with this new perspective, the material world was regarded as an essential aspect of divine consciousness. The body and its senses could actually be used as a vehicle for connection with the divine.

Tantra opened the door for the inclusion of sensory and body-based meditation practices. The senses were regarded as *devis*, or goddesses, who needed to be nourished. More subtle body practices involving sound and visualizations were developed. Over time, this body-centric perspective led to the postural yoga practice called hatha yoga (from which the modern style of yoga called "hatha" took its name).

The tantric and hatha yogis were very mindful of the role that sexual energy played in the cultivation of our life essence, or *ojas*. They developed practices to conserve, build, and harness this bodily energy, including increasing sexual energy without orgasm.

Given our modern culture, brahmacharya does not have to be interpreted as a prescription for chastity. However, it is an invitation to be aware of the power of our own sexuality and to use it wisely. In our culture, sexuality has been commodified and used as a marketing tool to sell everything from beer to cars. Casual sex has been glorified, and the misuse of sexual energy and power has been exposed in almost every aspect of contemporary culture, including yoga.

Brahmacharya invites us to explore our personal relationship with this powerful part of our nature, so that we can be aware of its potential and use it with awareness.

Consider the following:

▶ Do your sexual relationships serve you (this includes your sexual relationship with yourself)?

▶ Are you depleted or nourished in your relationship to your sexual energy?

▶ If you have a partner(s), how are they served by the relationship?

More broadly, brahmacharya invites you to investigate how you are replenishing, conserving, and using your vital energy in all areas of your life.

REFLECTION

▶ What activities do you find energetically depleting?

▶ What activities do you find nourishing?

▶ On the whole, how is your energy?

▶ What self-care practices can you use to refill your own energetic well?

13. PLEASURE

Raga

The Chariot Story (adapted from the Katha Upanishad)

Once upon a time, there was a chariot being pulled by five horses named Smell, Sight, Hearing, Taste, and Touch. Excited by everything around them, those horses ran after whatever new and delicious experience came across their path.

Carrots! Hay! The wind!

The horses' desire to pursue pleasure didn't make them bad horses; they were simply following the call of their nature.

There was a charioteer at the reins, named the mind. If the charioteer wasn't paying proper attention, the horses would race in every direction. But when the charioteer was present, the horses could be steered with intention.

However, the chariot only really got where it was supposed to go when the charioteer listened to the chariot's passenger, the soul. When the mind listened to the soul, then the chariot found its way to the proper destination.

We are wired for pleasure. In Sanskrit, pleasure is called *raga*. It is quite natural that our senses will pull us toward objects that bring pleasure. In sutra 2.7, Patanjali writes, "Attachment is a residue of a pleasant experience." From a neurological point of view, we seek to repeat experiences that fire up our brain's pleasure center.

However, our senses and our lower mind, *manas*, don't have consciousness. They are part of the "mind layer" of our experience *(manomaya kosha)* and lack discrimination and discernment. Left to pursue their own desires, our senses will indulge again and again in what brings them pleasure, whether it's wine, sugar, sex, or chocolate.

We may also use pleasure inappropriately, in order to cover up feelings of unworthiness, anxiety, sadness, or wanting. After all, it can seem far easier to reach for the glass of wine or tub of ice cream than to sit in our uncomfortable feelings.

Manas: mind

Manomaya kosha: the mind layer

"[Manomaya kosha is] where the incessant thoughts of human life occur."

—B.K.S. Iyengar, *Light on Life*

As the chariot story tells us, only when our highest self (our soul, purusha, self, witness) directs the horses do we truly move in the direction that serves our highest good.

Pleasure has always been a thorny issue for humankind. Early yogis chose to avoid the temptations of pleasure entirely, choosing instead to practice celibacy, fasting, and cleansing to avoid the distraction of pleasure. Many spiritual traditions have followed (and continue to follow) a similar path, preaching celibacy and advocating for the control or even suppression of the body.

The development of tantric yoga heralded a worldview that considered our bodies, our senses, and the world as the living fabric of the divine. Pleasure, at last, had a place in the spiritual human experience. Rather than be avoided and shunned, pleasure was recognized as an essential and valuable component of human experience.

> "We must increase our tolerance for pleasure."
>
> —Gil Hedley, PhD

However, tantric yogis also recognized that engaging in pleasure required a more sophisticated level of consciousness: the greater the pleasure, the more mindful we need to be. Creating a relationship with pleasure is far more challenging in some ways than avoiding it entirely. Perhaps you've experienced this for yourself: it can be easier to eliminate a pleasurable item entirely than to try to enjoy something in moderation.

Once we start to enjoy something — sugar, alcohol, cigarettes, sex, spending money, watching TV, gambling, engaging in social media — it can be hard for us to stop. Some pleasures are hard to control.

As yogis, our work is to become aware of our relationship to pleasure so that we may enjoy sensual delights fully and with integrity. Pleasure, sensuality, and beauty are birthrights of our human experience. Experiencing the warmth of sunshine, taking a deep breath, touching the softness of cashmere, and tasting delicious food are all gifts of our embodiment. Through mindfulness, we can increase our awareness of the pleasures in the present moment, and create a positive relationship with our sensual side.

PRACTICE

Eat one thing slowly:

▶ Choose a small amount of food that you really love. It could be something like a piece of chocolate, a raisin, a small piece of pizza, a strawberry. (preferably something that won't melt).

▶ Pause.

▶ Take in the food first with all of your senses except taste.

▶ After you have thoroughly explored it with your other senses, then very slowly, take a small bite.

▶ Roll it in your mouth to explore its texture, its different flavors.

▶ Give yourself over to the pleasure of the experience.

▶ Chew it many times.

▶ Slowly, small bite by small bite, begin to eat the food.

When you are finished, reflect:

▶ How was that experience different from your habitual approach to this food?

▶ How could this inform a new relationship to pleasure?

REFLECTION

- ▶ What is my current relationship to pleasure?
- ▶ Where can I make the time to experience pleasure in its fullest spectrum?
- ▶ Where and why do I not permit myself to experience pleasure?
- ▶ Where and why do I lose control and overindulge?
- ▶ When do I use pleasure to cover up uncomfortable feelings?
- ▶ Are there beliefs around pleasure I could revisit?

14. CONFLICT

Jnana Yoga

How can we be yogis, and engage in conflict? For most of us, the idea of engaging in violence and practicing yoga seem diametrically opposed. How can we resolve this seeming contradiction?

This paradox was one of the core issues explored in the great yogic text, the Bhagavad Gita. In the Gita, the warrior Arjuna is about to begin a great battle with his family. Although Arjuna is in the right, he can't fathom how killing his own family could possibly lead to any good. He throws down his weapons in despair and will not fight.

Like us, Arjuna is stuck. He realizes that he should take action, and yet can't abide the consequences that his actions will cause. We all know what it's like to be stuck between a rock and a hard place.

Soon after I was married, my spouse became despondent because his mother had died and he began drinking. Unfortunately, he also suffered from alcoholism. As time went on, he became emotionally abusive and I became increasingly enabling and withdrawn. I felt trapped between my commitment as a wife and friend and my growing unhappiness. I didn't know what to do.

Although the "right choice" in this scenario may seem more clear to me now, in the moment I felt consumed by doubt and indecision.

You have certainly experienced your own "rock and a hard place" moment, perhaps at work, with kids, with family, or in romantic relationships. As yogis who live in the world (rather than retreating to a cave for meditation), we will naturally be embroiled in the drama and chaos of daily life and conflict. So how do we choose what to do?

In the Bhagavad Gita, Arjuna is being advised by his charioteer, Krishna, who also (fortunately!) happens to be a god. Krishna represents the voice of our highest inner wisdom, or *buddhi*.

To help Arjuna navigate his situation, Krishna offers him three paths to insight: jnana yoga, karma yoga, and bhakti yoga. Although these three forms of yoga are slightly different, they are united by one guiding principle: *View the situation from the highest perspective.*

When we are debating a choice in our minds, we are always going to be stuck in competing stories. Should I do this? Should I do that? Our minds can justify any decision or point of view, so we will be left in confusion. Listening to just our feelings can provide some information, though fear or discomfort can distort them. Instead of making a decision based on thoughts and feelings, we must attune to the voice of our highest self, and be guided by our highest values.

In jnana yoga, the yoga of wisdom, we practice pausing so that we can step out of the tumult of thoughts and feelings, and return to a deeper, guiding sense of presence.

We can do this through a simple process:

▶ Pause.

- Take a few deep, slow breaths.
- Begin to observe your thoughts and feelings.
- Create space for all your thoughts and feelings to arise, be felt, and then dissipate or change.
- Begin to be the witness of what is arising for you.
- Be the space beyond the thoughts, rather than the thoughts.
- Be the space beyond the feelings, rather than the feelings.
- Stand in the space of the witness, rather than the story.

From this higher perspective, we can recognize our own intrinsic wholeness and a consistent sense of deep presence. When we are connected to self, we remember that we are fundamentally safe and are not as attached to things turning out a certain way. We know that we are okay—and we know that (in the case of relationship) the other will also be okay. Much of the drama that happens in our heads is because we have misguided attachment to a circumstances that must change. From this place, we can more easily see the highest path forward.

In the Bhagavad Gita, Arjuna eventually goes into battle. However, he is not going into battle for the sake of his ego, for material gain, or because he is emotionally reactive. He engages in battle because it is the highest action he can take to support justice and uphold his values.

Like Arjuna, when we feel we must do battle, our first job is to pause, connect more deeply with ourselves, and become clear on our highest values. We cannot avoid conflict, but we can do our best to make sure that we are entering the battlefield for the best reasons.

REFLECTION

Reflect upon and observe your own relationship to conflict:

▶ What is my relationship to conflict?

▶ Do I engage in battle for petty, selfish, or ego-centered reasons? If so, why? What do I perceive that I will gain? Is it true?

▶ Do I shrink from conflict, even when for the highest good? If so, why? What do I perceive that I will gain? Is it true?

▶ How can I support myself to be a spiritual warrior?

15. CONNECTION AND LOVE

Bhakti Yoga

Have you ever noticed that when you feel happy, safe, and full of love, you are naturally more compassionate, generous, energetic, and kind to others?

The nature of the world is love. One of the forms of yoga that Krishna imparted in the Bhagavad Gita, bhakti yoga, is the yoga of devotion, in which practitioners love their way into their highest self.

Try this:

▶ Pause and take a comfortable set.

▶ Close your eyes and take a few slow, deep breaths.

▶ Give yourself the space of a minute or so to notice the thoughts and feelings that arise.

▶ After a minute, bring to mind the face of someone you love unconditionally. This could be a person (living or deceased), but could also be a beloved pet.

▶ See their face, study their aspect, and allow the feelings you have for this creature to arise within you.

▶ After a minute or so, allow your visualization of the beloved to be released.

▶ Notice how you feel now. What has changed?

When we are in contact with a personal beloved (this doesn't need to be romantic love), we are connected with the essence of our own human heart. We experience softness, kindness, vulnerability, and we can more easily experience the good in others.

We can then extend this feeling of beneficence and goodwill beyond our personal beloved and begin to experience the essence and interconnectedness of the greater world. Not only our human communities, but we can also feel the divine interconnection of nature and all creatures everywhere.

We can also start with an appreciation for the magnificence of the divine, and allow that love to infuse the smallest details of our daily lives. Every act becomes an expression of devotion, reverence, and love. To the bhakti yogi, everything is an expression of the divine.

From the perspective of bhakti yogis, everything is connected. When we see the interconnectedness of all things, we can begin to love others as we love ourselves. And if we struggle with self-love, our increasing ability to see the beauty in others will allow us—as a reflection—to see the magnificence in ourselves.

"May all beings everywhere be happy and free."

Lokah Samastah Sukhino Bhavantu

—Sanskrit mantra

PRACTICE

▶ Take a comfortable seat.

▶ Take a few deep breaths and close your eyes.

▶ Focus on your breath.

▶ Bring to mind the face of someone you love. Take a few moments to imagine their details or how they make you feel.

▶ Think, Just like me, you want to be happy. Repeat this until you feel it.

▶ Bring to mind the face of someone you are neutral about. Take a few moments to imagine their details or how they make you feel.

▶ Think, Just like me, you want to be happy. Repeat this until you feel it.

▶ Bring to mind the face of someone with whom you may have challenges. Take a few moments to imagine their details or how they make you feel.

▶ Think, Just like me, you want to be happy. Repeat this until you feel it.

▶ Imagine that you could encompass the whole world in your meditation: Just like me, you want to be happy.

▶ When you are ready, take a few deep breaths and experience what you feel.

- ▶ What is my relationship to self-love?

- ▶ What are the obstacles to loving myself, or to loving others?

- ▶ Where (or for whom) do I feel unconditional love and devotion?

- ▶ How can I practice experiencing this love so that I can love others and myself more freely and with wonderful abandon?

16. NONVIOLENCE, COMPASSION

Ahimsa

In *The Yoga Sutras*, Patanjali shares an eight-limbed path called ashtanga yoga, which details eight components of the spiritual life. You can imagine these eight limbs as the roots of a tree, each one nourishing and sustaining the whole.

The first limb is called the *yamas*, which can be translated as "external disciplines." There are five yamas, each of which directs us in how to interact with the external world with integrity.

The first yama is *ahimsa*, which can be translated as "nonviolence." In Chip Hartranft's translation of sutra 2.35, Patanjali shares that "Being firmly grounded in nonviolence creates an atmosphere in which others can let go of their hostility."

Have you ever noticed that it "takes two to tango" where conflict is concerned? When we are able to relate to others from a space of compassion, rather than opposition, we can usually navigate our relationships with more grace.

Our anger usually emerges when the way the world is and the way we want the world to be are not aligned. We feel that the power of our anger (frustration, irritation, or rage) will somehow change the world more to our liking.

Although such emotions are natural, they usually result from a fundamental confusion: we have mistakenly vested our sense of self with the constantly changing world, rather than identifying with our true nature. In this confusion, we believe that our sense of safety and wholeness is associated with something outside of ourselves. For example, we identify strongly with our jobs, or our identity as a good worker or good dad. When these identities and stories are threatened, we rear up and fight back. Anger is always protective in nature, and emerges when we want to put the world back to rights.

However, if we were truly grounded and settled within ourselves, we would have no need to fight for anyone else's good opinion. Our own sense of wholeness would require no external affirmation or defense.

However, learning to identify with our core self—rather than the stories in our minds—takes practice. Practice, or *abhyasa*, is a continual, resilient, and loving intent to recognize that our true identity is the presence that lies beyond our thoughts and feelings, beyond our stories and reactions.

Rather than think about yamas—and ahimsa—as ethical guidelines to follow, you can instead think of them as signposts that you are on the right path. When we are correctly identified with our true nature (our presence, rather than the stories in our minds), we are less likely to get angry over something not working out the way we want.

We don't need to *try* to be non-violent; as we practice our yoga, we will become naturally more compassionate because the need to defend our egos will gradually start to drop away.

REFLECTION

▶ When do you express violence toward yourself? This can take the form of nonacceptance, judgment, or criticism.

▶ When you are angry, consider what you are trying to protect. Does it really need protecting?

Wherever you are, be there totally.

— Eckhart Tolle

17. TRUTHFULNESS

Satya

Have you ever had to keep a secret?

In one of my relationships, I wanted children, and my partner did not. Every time we spoke of the issue, we would find ourselves at a stalemate. Rather than face the huge elephant in the room and make the necessary changes, we instead began to live inside a bubble of denial and deceit.

The relationship was unsustainable. Every moment between us was weighed down by the heaviness of what was unspoken and we both grew increasingly unhappy. Through admitting the truth was very painful, it ultimately brought us clarity and peace.

> "The truth will set you free."
> —John 8:32

In *The Yoga Sutras*, the first limb of an eight-limbed path of yoga is called the *yamas*, which can be translated as "external disciplines." There are five yamas; the first yama is ahimsa, or non-violence, and the second yama is *satya*, or truthfulness. Patanjali writes in sutra 2.36, "For those grounded in truthfulness, every action and its consequences are imbued with truth" (translation, Chip Hartranft).

When we lie, our minds become anxious and divided. The lie demands that we remember what we have said, and give energy to maintaining its story. It can be hard for us to remain present and open when we have to devote energy to maintaining a fiction.

When we are truthful, we can more easily remain steady and clear. In our truthfulness, we empower others around us to live their truth as well.

Have you ever noticed that sometimes a hard conversation is worse to anticipate than to actually have? Dishonesty undermines authentic connection. When we are honest—even when it's hard—true connection is possible. Even when the truth leads to an honest willingness to "agree to disagree" (as can happen in my family's political conversations), truthfulness allows us to become more intimate and loving with others because we come out of hiding.

But if telling the truth is such a good idea, then why do we lie?

When I was a little girl, I used to respond to new information by pretending I already knew it. "I know," I'd reply, to any new tidbit. Being a little girl, I didn't understand a lot, so I was saying, "I know," a lot! My dad finally took my aside, and said, "You don't have to say that you know. It's okay not to know."

I remember feeling caught off guard. I had been saying, "I know," because I thought that knowing stuff would make me look good. Not knowing felt vulnerable and scary. While I could pretend that lying to save face was simply a little girl's folly, fast-forward 40 years and I'm still tempted to avoid admitting I don't know things.

One of my acquaintances cheated on his wife for eight years. Rather than have an honest conversation about his unhappiness, he thought it was kinder to leave her in the dark. She'd be so hurt, he justified to himself, and my kids would be devastated. Although both of these things may have been true, his primary motivation for lying was to protect himself from dealing with their disappointment. He didn't want to face the consequences of speaking his truth, and so he chose to lie for almost a decade.

Lying isn't only about what you say; it can also be about what you don't say.

For example, it's a common practice to "ghost" someone in the dating world, where one party disappears without further communication. She'll get it eventually, the ghoster may think, as he deletes his date's text message. But in the meantime, the other person has been left in the dark, wasting time thinking that the relationship may go somewhere. Rather than share an honest and immediate (if uncomfortable) accounting of their feelings, ghosters leave dates to linger in uncertainty for days.

We often tell ourselves that we are lying to protect someone else. But in reality, we almost always lie to protect ourselves. Here's the tricky part: embracing truthfulness isn't as simple as blurting out everything we're feeling and thinking.

As the yamas suggest, honesty rests in the gracious arms of compassion. Without compassion, blunt honesty can be needlessly hurtful and self-serving. To live satya in our lives, we must pause to consider if our expression of the truth is serving the greatest good. Is it needed? Is it helpful? When the truth can't help, then silence may be the most compassionate course. But if the truth will honor the personhood of someone else, then it may be our responsibility to share it.

One of the hardest moments of my life was telling my ex-husband that I wasn't in love with him anymore. I did not share this information to be cruel; I shared it with him so that he could move on in his own best interests and find a new relationship that would be fulfilling. I said it so that we would both be free.

Rather than think about yamas—and satya—as ethical rules, you can also think of them as signposts that you are on the right path. When we are correctly identified with our true nature (our Presence, rather than the stories in our minds), we are less likely to feel the need to protect our ego by creating fabrications or distorting the truth.

REFLECTION

▶ What is your relationship to speaking your truth?

▶ What gets in the way of you communicating honestly?

▶ Are there areas in your life in which you would like to create more honesty and truthfulness?

18. WHY WE FORGET

The Five Acts

You go to yoga class, experience a profound sense of peace and a loving appreciation for everyone around you. Then on the way home, someone cuts you off in traffic. "You idiot!" you holler. And just like that, divine connection goes *poof*.

If our true nature is to be one with the universe, then why do we keep forgetting ourselves so often?

According to tantric text, *The Heart of Recognition*, written by Rajanaka Kshemaraja around 1000 CE, the Divine is constantly performing five acts. And because we are part of the divine fabric, we are also constantly performing these five acts:

▶ The first act, *srsti*, is the act of creation. Through this act, the divine manifests into form. This could be the manifestation of anything: thought, a flower, or a human.

▶ The second act, *sthiti*, is stasis. Through this act, something holds its form.

▶ The third act, *samhara*, is reabsorption. Through this act, what has been in form is reabsorbed back into consciousness.

▶ The fourth act, *tirodhana*, is concealment. Through this act, the divine conceals its nature, or its qualities.

▶ The final and fifth act is *anugraha*, or revelation, through which the divine is revealed.

Tirodhana helps explain why we are constantly forgetting our true nature. Concealment is an essential aspect in the play of the divine. This act explains why we may experience glimpses of grace *(anugraha)*, only to find our understanding veiled once again.

The five acts are enormously comforting. It's as if the text lovingly puts a hand on our shoulder and whispers, "It's okay to forget, that's part of your journey, too."

REFLECTION

▶ What does it mean for you if the third act, samhara, does not mean "ending" or "death," but "reabsorption"?

▶ What is your typical reaction to your own forgetting?

▶ What activities allow you to reconnect with the fifth act, revelation?

19. STICKINESS

Asteya | Aparigraha

Have you ever gotten exactly what you wanted, only to be quickly dissatisfied and then have a hard time letting it go again? Our tendency to want something—then hold it tightly to us—is very human.

As a tangible example, my mom and dad have very different ideas about holding on to material possessions. My dad rolls his eyes at the accumulation of stuff in the garage, while my mother gasps in outrage. "You can't get rid of that," she'd say. "Rachel wore that dress when she was seven at her second-grade graduation!" For my mother, these physical items bring her a sense of security and emotional connection. For me, I may not hold on to physical stuff too tightly, but I relentlessly hold on to people. I have a very hard time ending relationships and letting people go, even though some ebb and flow is a natural part of the world's cycles.

Have you ever noticed a desire to hold on to something—whether it's clothing, a house, a job, money, or a relationship—even when it no longer serves you? We can get stuck holding on to less tangible objects, such as habits, reputations, ideas, or grudges. Yogis call this tendency "grasping." Our grasping creates a sticky quality, when we become attached to things working out just the way that we want so that we can look and feel good.

When we grasp, we attach our sense of identity or security to something

"For those who have no inclination to steal, the truly precious is at hand."

—Sutra 2.37

"Freedom from wanting unlocks the real purpose of existence."

—Sutra 2.39

outside of us. We mistakenly believe that holding on to the external object, idea, or person will bring us safety and worthiness.

This is an example of avidya, or the "great mistake." When we make the great mistake, we forget that worthiness and groundedness can only be found inside us. When we pause, breathe, and go inside, we find a true connection to our wholeness that is resilient and unchanging. From this space, we can let go of trying to control the world around us.

In *The Yoga Sutras*, Patanjali outlines external observances for relating to the world. These include non-stealing *(asteya)* and non-grasping *(aparigraha)*.

PRACTICE

▶ Come into a comfortable, tall seat.

▶ Soften your face, throat, and eyes.

▶ Take a few slow breaths.

▶ What if nothing needed to be different, right now?

▶ What would it feel like to be free from wanting?

REFLECTION

▶ Have you ever wanted to take something? (In addition to a physical object or money, this could include someone's time or ideas.)

▶ Why have you felt "sticky" about something (a person, object, idea, etc.)?

▶ What do you feel you are protecting by controlling that thing?

▶ What were you trying to gain from holding on to it?

▶ Consider a time in the past that you felt attached to something or someone. What was the result?

▶ Consider a time that you let something go. What was the result?

20. SADNESS AND DISCONNECTION

Anava Mala

According to tantric philosophy, you are a wondrous expression of the unfolding of divine universal consciousness. At its core, there is no separation between self and other, and we are all one.

So, if we're so great, why do we feel so bad?

At the core of human existence, is a fundamental sense of restlessness, emptiness, or longing. Tantric yogis call this feeling of incompleteness *anava mala*, and it is related to our hearts. Anava mala is one of the three core misperceptions that keep us from recognizing our own worthiness. Rather than remember our connection to our source, we often feel anxious, lacking, sad, and disconnected.

Because of anava mala, we try to fill this "inner hole" with resources from the external world. To feel better, we may engage is tactics like buying stuff, taking a prestigious job, eating ice cream, or clinging to unfulfilling romantic relationships. A good friend of mine often jokes that she likes to "eat her feelings." In addition to eating my own feelings (or occasionally drinking them) when I feel sad or lost, I overwork. Accomplishing something gives me the sense that I deserve to be loved. But soon enough, the glow of achievement wears off, and I'm scampering for the popcorn, wine, or to-do list to feel okay.

No matter how much we shore up our experience with stuff outside of us, this feeling of lack is simply part of being human, and it can only be truly filled through patient inner work.

In a way, this is excellent news because we no longer have to worry that something is wrong with us when we feel lost or sad. The even better news: these feelings of unworthiness are a misperception, not reality. When we feel this inner restlessness, we can smack our own foreheads and think, "Ah-ha! There's anava mala, at it again." We can then take a deep breath and devote time to reconnecting to our own inner resources.

PRACTICE

▶ Come into a comfortable, tall seat.

▶ Soften your face, throat, and eyes.

▶ Close your eyes.

▶ Take a few slow, deep breaths.

▶ Notice the rising and falling of your thoughts and feelings.

▶ Allow all the thoughts and feelings to have space to come and go. (Crying in meditation is just fine.)

▶ Notice that, given space and presence, even intense feelings will shift and change into something else.

- ▶ Connect to the space that is watching these sensations arise: your presence (or self, or witness).
- ▶ From this inner space beyond the thinking, in this moment, is anything really lacking?

REFLECTION

- ▶ How do you usually try to fill your inner feeling of scarcity? What are your favorite tactics?

- ▶ As you move through the day, can you catch yourself before you try to fill the void? We're usually so good at avoiding this inner feeling that we cover it up before we even notice it. Try to pause and stay in the uncomfortable feeling for 10 breaths before "fixing" it.

- ▶ As you experience your sensations, thoughts, and feelings, can you also connect to the presence that holds space for all of these experiences?

21. COMPARISON AND JEALOUSY

Mayiya Mala

There's a saying: "A rich man is the one who earns five dollars more than his neighbor."

We continually compare ourselves to others, jockeying to see if we measure up. We compare everything: our appearance, success, good fortune, likeability—the list goes on and one. Our culture, rooted in competition and capitalism, encourages these judgmental feelings. Standards for beauty and achievement are impossible to meet. When we compete with Photoshop beauty and celebrity wealth, it's hard to look good by comparison. And our constant feeling of lack makes the economic world go round; after all, the best marketing creates a need you didn't know you had, then sells you the solution to fix it!

Given that someone out there will always be prettier, richer, thinner, and more successful, how are we supposed to feel good about ourselves?

According to tantric yoga, this feeling of separateness and comparison is called *mayiya mala*. Related to the mind, it is one of three core misperceptions that keep us from recognizing our connection to everything around us. In the tantric worldview, we are all part of one divine whole. Given that we spend so much time labeling and differentiating things, this may seem a little counterintuitive. But it all depends on your point of view. If you imagine the world from the point of view of quantum physics, we are all immersed in a seething, connected form of particles. In the same way, the tantra affirm that — despite the seeming differences — we're part of one continuity from the highest perspective.

To account for the seeming differences, tantra recognizes forces at play that keep us from recognizing our intrinsic connection. Mayiya mala creates the experience of subject and object, where I perceive myself as being separate from you. Once that happens, then the comparisons start. This confusion leads to feelings of jealousy, anger, and unworthiness.

The good news: it's normal to feel this way. Mayiya mala is an intrinsic part of the universal order. The even better news: if we practice reconnecting to our true nature, then the apparent separations between us and everything else will start to dissolve.

....

"A human being is a part of the whole, called by us universe, a part limited in time and space. He experiences himself, his thoughts, and feelings as something separated from the rest — a kind of optical delusion of his consciousness. This delusion is a kind of prison for us, restricting us to our personal desires and to affection for a few persons nearest to us. Our task must be to free ourselves from this prison by widening our circle of compassion to embrace all living creatures and the whole of nature in its beauty."

—Albert Einstein

....

PRACTICE FOR RECOGNITION OF INTERCONNECTION

▶ Take a comfortable seat.

▶ Take a few deep breaths and close your eyes.

▶ Focus on your breath.

▶ As you do, begin to notice that the air you are breathing connects you intimately with the outer world.

▶ With every inhale, you bring the world into you (oxygen from trees, plants, etc.).

▶ With every exhale, you give back to the world.

▶ Can you extend your vision, imagining the collective breathing of all the humans, plants, and animals around you?

▶ Feel your participation with the great breath of the earth.

PRACTICE FOR RECOGNITION OF PERSPECTIVE

▶ Take a comfortable seat.

▶ Take a few deep breaths and close your eyes.

▶ Consider another person who has caused you to experience jealousy.

- ▶ For a moment, indulge in all the feelings of comparison that come up for you.
- ▶ After a minute, let that go and take a few deep breaths.
- ▶ Consider this person again.
- ▶ This time, focus on all your similarities (experiences, passions, vulnerabilities, physical similarities — anything).
- ▶ Stay with this contemplation for a few minutes.
- ▶ How did that feel?

REFLECTION

- ▶ When and why do I find myself comparing myself with others?
- ▶ What do I get out of being "better"?
- ▶ What do I get out of being "worse"?
- ▶ What practices help me find connection rather than disconnection?

22. WHY IS MY MIND SO CRAZY?

Parts of the Mind

Does your mind sometimes spin out of control?

The good news is that you're in very good company. The even better news is that yogis have been studying the mind for thousands of years. By understanding how the mind works, we are better equipped to use the mind as a tool, rather than let it run the show.

We all have voices in our heads that are all vying for control. By identifying "who" is talking, we can determine who to put in the driver's seat.

Here are the major players:

▶ Sense organs: allow you to sense the world around you through touch, hearing, sight, smell, and taste.

▶ *Manas*, the "lower mind," pulls together sensory information and compiles it to create an experience of the world.

▶ *Ahamkara*, the ego, or "I-maker," helps us to distinguish ourselves from the world around us. (I am happy, I am sad, I am a good person, I am an architect, I am a yogi, I am a mother, etc.).

> "The mind is a wonderful servant but a terrible master."
> —Robin Sharma

Ahamkara attaches our sense of self to an experience.

▶ *Smrti*, one of the *vrittis* (fluctuations of the mind and memor) is the storehouse of our past impressions and experiences and can provide information for how to navigate the present moment. Left on autopilot, smriti will create reactions based on past experiences.

▶ *Buddhi*, higher mind, is the voice of discrimination *(viveka)* and is connected to your higher self.

To illuminate the different parts of our minds, consider this story:

You're finishing up a long day of work and are tired. Your body feels sore, lethargic, and stiff (sense organs). I'm tired, you think (ego). You open the freezer and see (sense organ) a frozen pizza. It's your roommate's and she's out of town. She's told you to have whatever you like (memory).

Inside your mind, your ego and your memory have a quick confab. Do I like pizza? your ego asks your memory. Yes!, memory replies.

Yay! says ego, and tells your hand to grab the pizza.

Wait!, shouts a new voice. Ego and memory turn around to see buddhi running forward. They regard buddhi suspiciously because buddhi isn't always the most fun person at the party.

Memory buddhi asks, What happens after you eat pizza? Memory pauses and shuffles its feet a bit, but is willing to answer honestly and thoroughly when asked the right question: I don't tolerate gluten or cheese very well, and I feel bloated and my tummy hurts.

Zen is not an art, it's not a religion. It's a realization.

—Gene Clark

So should we really eat this pizza? Buddhi asks. After all, there's also a nice salad in the fridge.

Ego stamps its feet. But I worked hard and I deserve it! I need to have some pleasure in my life! Waaaaaaaaaahhhhh! And ego throws a temper tantrum.

Buddhi finally says sharply, Ego, get a grip! You know you feel like crap after eating pizza, and you've been whining lately about how your yoga pants feel tight. So stop whining already and leave the pizza alone!

And under the influence of buddhi, they step away from the pizza, and decide to have the nice salad after all. And after eating, ego smugly says, I'm so glad that I made that smart decision. I was right all along.

REFLECTION

► Which part of your mind is usually in the driver's seat?

► How can you tell which part of your mind is talking to you?

► What practices can you undertake so that buddhi has room to share its point of view?

23. FOR SURRENDER

Isvara Pranidhana

Sometimes, you have to let go.

In *The Yoga Sutras*, Patanjali outlines three components to kriya yoga, the yoga of action.

Tapas can be literally translated as "heat." Swami Satchidananda translates it as "accepting pain as help for purification," but I prefer the definition, "the willingness to endure intensity for the sake of transformation. Tapas incites us to engage our willpower, fire up our effort, and to embrace discomfort to move forward.

Svadhyaya is self-study, the willingness to frankly and deeply look at ourselves.

And the third component, *isvara pranidhana* — the yoga of action — is a willingness to surrender to the highest.

Tapah svadhyayesvara pranidhanani kriya yogah

"Accepting pain as help for purification, study of spiritual books, and surrender to the Supreme Being constitute Yoga in practice."

—Sutra 2.1

For many of us, surrender is the most challenging aspect of kriya yoga. In a world that demands achievement, independence, and forward movement, it can seem easier to embrace discomfort than to practice letting go. We are taught that we are the architects of our destiny, but this fails to accommodate for circumstances that arise beyond our control.

Learning to let go is not the same thing as giving up. Recognizing the limits of our personal responsibility is not the same thing as relinquishing accountability. There comes a point when we have done what we can, and our only next step is to "let go and let God." When we surrender to the highest, we are mindfully giving our trust over to something greater than ourselves.

PRACTICE

▶ Take time each day to focus lightly on your breath.

▶ Sit quietly and then let yourself feel your breath moving in and out of your body.

▶ Give yourself over to your body's natural rhythm and trust your innate intelligence.

REFLECTION

▶ What is my relationship to surrender?

▶ What is my relationship to control?

▶ What do I lose by letting go?

▶ What do I gain?

▶ How did letting go in the past turn out?

24. PURIFICATION

Sauca

Cleaning out closets, engaging in a juice fast, avoiding sugar, unplugging from technology are all examples of *sauca*, or "purification." Purification practices help us to create clarity and simplicity. When our lives feel overloaded—with material stuff or too much to do—our minds can start running on the hamster wheel. Engaging in a purification practice helps us cleanse the distractions from our lives so that we can create a clear and more open space.

Practically speaking, it's hard to practice yoga or calm our minds when our bodies don't feel well. If we're recovering from a hangover, stressed out, or have eaten heavy food, it's harder to clear our minds and feel connected to our inner wholeness.

Through the practiced of sauca, we can become more conscious and caring stewards of our bodies, so that they can support us to live vibrant, sustainable lives.

PRACTICE

Engaging in purification practices can also take into account our mental and emotional health. In addition to physical practices, sauca practices could include the following:

- Clear your calendar.

- Fast from social media.

- Donate stuff you no longer use.

- Drink enough water.

- Have a good, cleansing sweat.

- Eat nourishing foods.

- Fast intermittently.

- Take space for yourself.

- Exercise.

- Get good rest.

- Speak honestly.

- Unplug from technology.

- Create good boundaries in relationships.

- Clear toxic energy from your life.

- Develop new, healthy habits.

REFLECTION

- ▶ Where in your life do you feel cluttered or overwhelmed?

- ▶ Where in your life would you like to create more simplicity or clarity?

- ▶ What is one small step you can take to make that change?

- ▶ Can you make any dietary changes that will serve your overall health?

25. CONTENTMENT

Santosha

What is your relationship to contentment?

Santosha is one of the *niyamas*, which are guidelines for relating more graciously with ourselves. Santosha invites us to practice "being with what is," rather than fighting constantly against the world. When we practice contentment, we begin to soften to the present moment. Finding the space to be, rather than do, allows us to receive and immerse ourselves in the world as it is. We drop our agendas, and stop trying to exact control on the circumstances — and people — around us. By giving ourselves space, we also give others room to be as they are.

When we are not content, we are often fighting to change the world. Although a wholesome zeal is healthy, focusing only on our goals means we can only see our own agenda. We're like a horse with blinders on; although helpful for getting to our destination, we may miss the sights and side routes along the way.

When we drop our control strategies, we can take in the vista of our whole experience and see outside the tunnel vision of our own wants and desires. We discover the small wonders of this present moment. Being present brings us many gifts — the air on our

> "Contentment brings unsurpassed joy."
>
> —Sutra 2.42

skin, the feel of our breath, the sound of the wind—that we may miss when we are focused on doing.

Contentment is the antidote of regret, or self-blame, which keeps us locked in the past. Regret is a way of trying to control our history; we believe that if we feel badly enough, we can somehow change something that already happened. When we blame ourselves for something—a relationship, a dream deferred, a misstep—we are looking back with 20/20 hindsight, rather than acknowledging that we did the best we could at the time. Blame keeps us locked in the drama of the experience. Although practicing contentment doesn't alleviate our accountability, it gives us the space to learn from what we did and move forward.

PRACTICE

You can practice this walking meditation seated if you prefer:

▶ Without a particular agenda or destination, go for a walk.

▶ As you do, immerse yourself in the sights and senses of the world around you.

▶ Can you experience the world just as it is, curious about what it will bring you?

REFLECTION

▶ In what areas of your life do you struggle with contentment? What are you protecting by not allowing things to be?

▶ A wonderful way to cultivate contentment is to start a daily gratitude practice by listing at least five things for which you are grateful.

▶ Write down any unresolved areas of self-blame from the past. What did you learn from experience that you treasure?

26. HAPPINESS AND SUFFERING

Avidya

Avidya, "non-seeing," is the fundamental obstacle to happiness and self-awareness. In sutra 2.5, Patanjali explains that avidya is seeing the impermanent as permanent, the impure as pure, and the non-self as the self.

Have you ever completely identified yourself with something, like a job, skill, or place you lived—and then lost it?

One of my friends was a professional Irish step dancer. She devoted her entire childhood and adolescence to her dance career. By the time she was 20, she had fractured both her shins and was no longer able to dance. She was devastated. Dancing was her life. Who was she, if not a dancer?

In this instance, she suffered from a case of mistaken identity. She had believed that something impermanent—her identity as a dancer, and the resilience of her body—was permanent. We all do this in some way. Perhaps you attach your sense of self-esteem to a job and your achievements, or to your appearance, health, or relationships. When these elements change—as they will and must—we feel as if the ground has fallen out from underneath us. Although it's normal, and part of the joy of being alive to experience and enjoy these things while we can, Patanjali cautions that we suffer when we become overly attached to things that will inevitably change. When we remember that they are impermanent, we can hold them more lightly. We can savor their ephemeral beauty rather than take them for granted.

PRACTICE

▶ Take a tall, comfortable seat.

▶ Enjoy a few deep, easy breaths.

▶ Watch your thoughts as they arise and dissipate.

▶ Rather than get caught up in the content, be an observer.

▶ Giving time and space for each question, consider:

  ▶ Who is the watcher? Who is looking out of your eyes?

  ▶ Five years ago, who was looking out of your eyes?

  ▶ Ten years ago, who was looking out of your eyes?

  ▶ When you were 10, who was looking out of your eyes?

  ▶ When you were a baby, who was looking out of your eyes?

This is the self.

REFLECTION

▶ When in the past have you suffered because you mistook the impermanent for permanent?

▶ Make a list of what is most important to you right now. Are these things permanent or impermanent?

▶ How might recognizing their impermanence make them more precious?

▶ Spend time in nature and notice the natural cycles around you that contain beginnings, middles, endings, and new beginnings.

27. SELF-STUDY

Svadhyaya

One of the components of kriya yoga (yoga of action) is *svadhyaya*, or self-study. Patanjali also lists svadhyaya as one of the niyamas, or internal observances.

Svadhyaya operates on two levels: becoming aware of our own conditioning, and recognizing our own true nature.

Becoming aware of our conditioning increases our accountability for how we navigate the world.

Before I was married, I didn't know how to engage in conflict. My ex-husband was much more accustomed to expressing what he wanted—vigorously and passionately. When my marriage encountered problems and he started getting loud, I shut down and went silent. Only through studying our dynamic over time did I realize I had a blind spot when it came to expressing myself in conflict.

We are only consciously aware of a small part of our conditioning. If you'd asked me before my marriage how I would be in an emotional and psychological conflict, I would have thought of myself as a strong,

Sva: self

Dhyaya: contemplate

grounded human who could hold her own. Personal circumstances, however, exposed a different and deeper pattern. Although this exposure was painful, this awareness enabled me to learn more about myself, and do the work to consciously learn a new communication pattern.

Think of yourself as an iceberg. Although you may have a conscious sense of the tip of your own iceberg, you are unconscious of the vast majority of the iceberg that glides beneath the surface. And clearly, what's beneath the water will determine how you operate and where you go. By watching how you interact with the world, you can begin to see your conditioning more clearly. Through the practice of svadhyaya, you can make conscious choices about how you want to relate to yourself and others.

Your conditioning is not your destiny; through the power of consciousness, you have the ability to make new choices that uphold who you want to be.

The second layer of svadhyaya is recognition of your own true nature. Becoming mindful of your conditioning can help you improve your behavior, but it will not necessarily support your spiritual liberation. If you think of your personality as a house that you live in, then evolving your conditioning is a little like renovating and redecorating your house. Liberation is like leaving the house entirely.

Spiritual liberation requires detangling your habitual identification of self with your ego/personality, and learning to recognize self as the consciousness and awareness that lies within you. Imagine you are a drop of water in the ocean; spiritual liberation involves recognizing your connection with the entire ocean. Practices such as meditation and studying spiritual books can help us to connect more deeply with the self as awareness.

REFLECTION

▶ What does your yoga practice reveal about you? (Do you tend to dial it back, or "push through"? Do you prefer movement or stillness? Music or silence?)

▶ What is the relationship between vulnerability and growth?

▶ When you encounter discomfort, what do you do?

▶ Reflect upon your day: What did your choices reveal about who you are?

▶ What are your go-to books for feeling connected and elevated?

28. DISLIKE

Dvesha

Where does dislike come from?

When I was in college, my roommate took me out for sushi. I'd never had sushi before and I hated the new tastes and textures. I couldn't understand what she liked about it and was very reluctant to try it again.

According to the yogis, the origin of aversion, or *dvesha*, is simple. We dislike something we associate with an unpleasurable experience.

Animals are often trained through stimulus response: if they get a treat, they repeat a behavior; if the response is negative, they will shun the behavior. Humans aren't any different: we generally want to avoid experiences that have been unpleasant. Over time, we accumulate a storehouse of memories that train our likes and dislikes. After all, you only have to touch a hot stove once.

"Aversion is that which follows identification with painful experiences."

—Sutra 2.8

Although learning to avoid danger is a survival skill, not all aversion is helpful. After all, going to the gym or having a hard conversation isn't pleasant, but it is good for us. Part of our yoga practice is to become aware of our learned conditioning so we may make conscious choices. When we recognize that our present perception is being filtered through a lifetime of previous experiences, we can be more alert to when the past falsely colors our point of view.

A few weeks after I had my first sushi experience, I tried it again. Turns out that I love sushi. If I hadn't been willing to test my assumptions about my initial aversion, I would have missed out on one of my favorite foods.

REFLECTION

- ▶ When a sense of aversion or dislike arises, become curious.
- ▶ Can you remember the first time you experienced this dislike?
- ▶ If the present moment were a clear slate, might you experience it differently?
- ▶ Do you have any aversions you wish to reframe or change?

29. FEAR OF CHANGE

Abhinivesa

Human nature abhors uncertainty. Even when change is for the better, we balk at changing our life. Our instinctive impulse to hunker down and endure is why many of us stay in relationships, jobs, and situations that don't really serve us or allow us to fully thrive.

I was in a relationship that made me very unhappy. When I spoke about my situation with my friends, breaking up was the obvious solution. But as soon as I started to take action, I became consumed by crippling panic. My logical mind crumpled in the anxiety that arose in the face of ending my relationship.

Abhinivesa is the fear of death. It reflects a primal desire to cling to what is habitual and to avoid change or loss. One of the obstacles *(kleshas)* to self-realization, abhinivesa is said to be powerful, even in the wise.

Find comfort in the fact that it is normal to be afraid of change. It's normal to want to hold on. It doesn't have to feel good to be right. Ending my relationship felt terrible, but ultimately it was the best thing to do.

> "Clinging to life is instinctive and self-perpetuating, even for the wise."
>
> —Sutra 2.9

When we are confronted with change, it's natural to want to freeze or change course. Rather than react, we can practice holding space for our discomfort. When we do, we may begin to recognize something within us that is whole and safe. When we connect with this steady sense of awareness, we anchor our awareness in a deeper connection that will help us to sustain the choices that align with our highest selves.

PRACTICE

▶ Come into a comfortable seat.

▶ Take a few deep, expansive breaths.

▶ As you settle, notice your thoughts and feelings.

▶ Allow them to come and go.

▶ Connect to the space of the witness, or observer, of your experience.

▶ From this perspective, are you safe in this moment?

▶ From this perspective, are you whole in this moment?

Be the change that
you want to see in
the world.

——Mahatma Gandhi

REFLECTION

▶ What is your emotional relationship to change?

▶ Consider a time when your world "fell apart." How did you navigate the chaos?

▶ Does anything in your life need to end? What has stood in the way?

▶ What practices support you to stay connected to a sense of safety and wholeness?

30. CULTIVATING STABILITY

Muladhara Chakra

Part of the subtle body system, chakras are places in the body where energy is particularly condensed. Although there are energy centers all through the body, the seven primary chakras run along the spine, from pelvis to crown. Each chakra is associated with a particular element: earth, water, fire, air, ether, light, thought. Earth is associated with the first chakra, and thought is associated with the seventh. (However, "higher" chakras aren't better; each is necessary for holistic health.) A modern view of the chakras assigns each governance over different aspects of our experience and assigns each chakra with a different psychological fundamental right.

Situated in the base of the pelvis, *muladhara* ("root") chakra governs our connection with physical reality, materialism, and our bodies. Not surprisingly, it is associated with the element earth and our right to physically exist. As the closest chakra to the ground, it physically relates to our pelvis, legs, and organs of elimination. Someone who has a strong connection to this element may be said to have their "feet on the ground," or "be grounded," or seem "anchored." They have a strong sense of their physical presence and aren't afraid to take up space.

But too much earth energy can lead to heaviness, lethargy, stubbornness, and inertia. Symptoms of excessive muladhara include physical heaviness, rigidity, hoarding, and materialism. Too little earth energy can be equally problematic; someone may be delusional, ungrounded, or have their "head in the clouds."

PRACTICE

▶ Hold standing yoga poses to cultivate stability in legs and pelvis.

▶ Practice yin yoga to focus on long holds for pelvis and legs.

▶ Do: squats and lunges to energize the legs and pelvis.

▶ Get out in nature.

▶ Stamp feet.

▶ Do visualizations.

▶ On inhale, imagine pulling energy from the center of the earth to the core of your pelvis.

▶ On exhale, send energy from your pelvis down into the earth.

REFLECTION

▶ What is my relationship to my physical body?

▶ How do I feel about "taking up space"?

▶ What is my relationship to material possessions?

▶ Do I have too much earth, too little, or do I feel balanced? If I'm out of balance, what could I do for self-care?

31. CULTIVATING FLOW

Svadhisthana Chakra

Svadhisthana ("sweetness") chakra is the energy center that governs our relationship with flow, sensuality, and our emotions, and is associated with our right to feel. Situated just below the navel, this chakra relates to our urinary and sexual organs (bladder, urethra, ovaries, uterus, prostrate, testicles, penis, vagina). A balanced relationship to this chakra is reflected in a healthy relationship to one's sensuality, sexuality, and feelings.

Svadhisthana is associated with the element water. Water invites a sense of flow, movement, receiving, and letting go. Water needs movement to be healthy; lack of healthy circulation leads to stagnation and disease. Our emotions and sensations are like water; they need space to be felt and to change.

Someone who may have an excess of this energy may have loose boundaries, have difficulty holding space, or feel overrun by their feelings. Someone who experiences a deficiency in this energy may suppress their feelings, be locked up or rigid, or be unavailable to the flow of sensual energy.

PRACTICE

▶ Do flow styles of yoga that focus on movement and breath.

▶ Do yin yoga/hip openers.

▶ Inspire the senses: enjoy eating a delicious food slowly, savoring a beautiful view, or enjoying the sensation of touching different textures.

▶ Slow down and take time to feel.

▶ Spend time emotional journaling and healing.

REFLECTION

▶ What is my relationship to my feelings?

▶ What is my relationship to my sensual nature?

▶ Would I be served by creating stronger boundaries, or do I want to invite more flow?

▶ Do I have too much water, too little, or do I feel balance? If I'm out of balance, what could I do for self-care?

32. CULTIVATING FIRE

Manipura Chakra

Located at the solar plexus, *manipura chakra* is an energy center controlled by the element of fire and is related to willpower and transformation. Manipura controls how we assert the ego in relationship to the world and is related to the right to take action.

Physically, manipura is related to digestion, where fire (acid, bile) is used to transform external material into sustenance. Similarly, manipura relates to our ability to emotionally "digest" and process our experiences.

When people have excessive fire energy, they may be controlling, overbearing, and arrogant. If they have too little fire energy, they may lack a sense of self and be overly accommodating.

PRACTICE

- ▶ Do hot yoga or power yoga.
- ▶ Focus on the abdomen with twists and core yoga poses.
- ▶ Focus on cardio or weights, heat building, core exercises, boxing or martial arts.
- ▶ Get a good sweat in a sauna.
- ▶ Focus intensely on one thing.
- ▶ Communicate needs and desires clearly.

REFLECTION

- ▶ What is my relationship to my own fire and sense of self?
- ▶ What is my relationship to my willpower?
- ▶ Am I able to assert my own needs, wants, and desires?
- ▶ Am I able to listen to others?
- ▶ Do I have too much fire, too little, or do I feel balanced? If I'm out of balance, what could I do for self-care?

33. GIVING AND RECEIVING LOVE

Anahata Chakra

Anahata chakra is our heart center and is located in the very middle of the chakra system. It is the midway point between the lower three chakras (relating to the energy of the material world) and the etheric elements (relating to energy of the spiritual world). Anahata is the bridge between the earth and sky and is associated with the right to love.

Anahata means "unstruck," which is a reminder that our innermost heart is pure, untouched, and free. Governed by air and movement, anahata is related physically to our lungs, heart, and arms. Anahata's energy is made physical through how we reach out and touch the world.

Anahata is about negotiating balance; our heart chakra governs how we both receive and express love, just as our lungs receive and exhale air. If we have too much air energy, we may lose ourselves in someone else, lack boundaries, and "give ourselves away." If we are lacking in this center, we may withhold love or be stingy in our loving expression. When healthy and in balance, anahata governs our ability to engage in healthy and nourishing exchange: to give as well as receive from others.

PRACTICE

- ▶ Do heart openers or side body-opening yoga poses.
- ▶ Pranayama opens the ribs and expands the breath.
- ▶ Focus on heart-centered meditations.
- ▶ Donate your time or energy to a good cause.
- ▶ Do acts of kindness for others.
- ▶ Create a list of everything and everyone you are grateful for.
- ▶ Observe the mystery of the world with awe on nature walks or in the night sky.

REFLECTION

- ▶ What is my relationship to my own heart?
- ▶ What is my relationship to self-love?
- ▶ Are there areas (or relationships) in my life where I feel out of balance in giving and receiving?
- ▶ Do I struggle to give, or do I struggle to receive?
- ▶ How can I make space to focus on my own needs?
- ▶ What practices can I use to self-care for my heart?

34. COMMUNICATION

Vishuddha Chakra

The throat chakra, *vishuddha* governs our self-expression and our right to speak. Located in the sternal notch, the element of vishuddha is ether and is physically related to our vocal cords, mouth, sinuses, and throat. Ether is the most refined of the five elements; with vishuddha, we have left the more visceral energies of the lower chakras and moved closer to the refined energy of consciousness.

Vishuddha governs our conscious self-expression. Although this energy may manifest in how we literally speak, it may also emerge in how we share our voice through our work, art, and hobbies.

When the energy in this chakra is excessive, we may talk incessantly and over-share a point of view. We might inundate our audience with words, and find it challenging to listen to others. When the energy of this center is undernourished, we may find it challenging to share ourselves authentically, find expression, or speak our truth. When vishuddha is well balanced, we are able to powerfully articulate who we are in the world, while at the same time leaving space for others to be heard.

PRACTICE

- ▶ Do chanting, mantra, kirtan.
- ▶ Try twists (turning head), fish, or shoulder stand.
- ▶ Sing or speak in public.
- ▶ Spend time writing creatively.
- ▶ Share your feelings in a safe space.
- ▶ Do expressive arts: painting, art, dance, free movement, acting, etc.

REFLECTION

- ▶ What is my relationship to my own communication?
- ▶ What is the quality of my speech?
- ▶ What is the quality of my listening?
- ▶ How can I nourish my own authentic expression?

35. VISION

Ajna Chakra

Located at our "third eye" between the eyebrows, *ajna chakra* is the energy center for visualization. Related to our optic nerve and our brain, the element of ajna is light and its right is to see. At the third eye, we have moved past the five gross elements (earth, water, fire, air, ether) of the first five chakras and now are firmly in the realm of etheric energy.

Ajna governs our vision and imagination. Humans have a rare and extraordinary ability to conceive of ideas, images, and metaphors beyond the realm of the five senses or the present moment. Our imagination enables us to problem solve and innovate beyond the bounds of our current knowledge, leading to technology, art, spirituality, science, and culture.

When this energy center is well balanced, we have a creative springboard to imagine new possibilities, create a vision for our future, and develop plans and goals that extend into the future. However, when this energy is excessive, we may get caught up in delusion, fantasy, anxiety, or paranoia. An uncontrolled mind may run wild with worry or distraction. When ajna chakra is deficient, then we may feel trapped in old ideas, habits, or conditioning.

PRACTICE

- ▶ Meditate and visualize.

- ▶ Do child's pose with forehead on a block.

- ▶ Do activities that stimulate the mind, like games, puzzles, riddles, math, or coloring books.

- ▶ Read elevating books.

- ▶ Entertain and debate new ideas.

- ▶ Create goals for the future, and visualize your ideal life.

- ▶ Enjoy cultural appreciation by listening to music, or visiting museums, ballet, theater, the symphony, etc.

REFLECTION

- ▶ What is my relationship to my own imagination?

- ▶ What is my relationship to my thoughts and the stories in my head?

- ▶ Am I able to manifest my ideas into reality?

- ▶ Am I open to dreaming new possibilities?

36. SPIRITUALITY

Sahasrara

The crown chakra, *sahasrara*, is the energetic center that governs our relationship with a higher spiritual power. Physically, this chakra is related to the brain, as well as the space above the head, and its right is to know. The most etheric of the chakras, this center's associated element is thought, and it enables us to step beyond the bounds of our individual identity to connect with universal consciousness. Through sahasrara, we participate in our relationship with the divine.

If we are excessive in this spiritual energy, we may not seem grounded in earthly reality. Someone who is connected to sahasrara without the stability of the more visceral chakras may be an otherworldly mystic or ascetic who leaves behind earthly energies to commune with their God. Someone who is deficient in this energy may not experience their connection to something bigger than themselves. They may find it hard to experience awe and wonder, or may feel shut off from spiritual connection.

Someone who is well balanced in this energy will be able to experience a rich and growing connection to the divine, while keeping their feet firmly rooted on the earth.

PRACTICE

- ▶ Meditate or visualize.

- ▶ Work on your headstand or headstand prep.

- ▶ Engage in elevating spiritual conversations.

- ▶ Read spiritual books.

- ▶ Listen to mantra.

- ▶ Engage in experiences that create awe and wonder, like nature walks or stargazing..

- ▶ Spend quiet time in introspection and self-inquiry.

REFLECTION

- ▶ What is my relationship to my spirituality?

- ▶ Where do I experience awe and wonder?

- ▶ How can I create more space for the divine in my daily life?

37. TRANSFORMATION AND ALCHEMY

Hatha Yoga

We might associate the word *hatha* with a softer style of yoga practice, but the word means "forceful." Historically, hatha is a school of yoga that developed in the Middle Ages. The goal for hatha yogis was to create an "adamantine" body that was strong enough to withstand the forces of transformation. To this end, they developed a rich array of body-based practices such as *asana* (postures), *pranayama* (breathing practice), *kriyas* (cleansing techniques), *mudra* (seals), *bandhas* (energetic locks), and *drishti* (gazing points) to cleanse, intensify, and focus the power of the body.

Hatha yoga emerged from the philosophical roots of tantric yoga, and was also influenced by the practice of alchemy. A forerunner to chemistry, practitioners of alchemy sought to transmute base metals and substances into precious and refined substances like gold. Although alchemists pursued this work literally, hatha yogis worked metaphorically to eradicate impurities in their bodies and minds. Thus purified, they were more easily able to enter states of meditation and connect with the absolute.

In this same way, our modern yoga practice is a process of conscious transformation. Every time we arrive at the mat, or our meditation seat, we deliberately create a sacred space in which to shift our experience. Some of these changes are physical (open hamstrings, stronger core), but the most profound shifts are mental, emotional, and spiritual.

As hatha yogis, we are the living continuation of this lineage. We are modern day alchemists, evolving and refining our lives with every practice.

REFLECTION

▸ What in your life right now requires transformation? (Consider attitude, material possessions, relationships, habits.)

▸ What will you gain?

▸ How can your practice (asana, pranayama, meditation, or mindfulness) support your transformation?

38. ANGER

Kali

Hindu philosophy is replete with epic tales of gods, goddesses, and magical creatures. Rather than be viewed literally as gods, they are metaphorical figures that provide relatable access points to the various aspects of the divine. Each figure has its own temperament and energetic qualities; by connecting to this aspect of the divine, the devotee is able to call up the essence of its energy.

The goddess Kali is the fierce, dark mother. She is terrifying in her aspect, having red eyes and wearing a necklace of severed heads. She is the most powerful aspect of the goddess, and is evoked when it is time for necessary destruction. Her anger is just, uncontrolled, and undefeatable. She is like a raging fire, purifying and destroying what is in its path to make way for a rebirth. Although Kali is fearsome, she is also worshipped for her fierce love and protection.

Ultimately, anger is protective in nature. It arises from a deep, passionate love to protect something beloved to us. Many of us have been taught to suppress our anger as "non-yogic" or not "nice." Kali reminds us that divine anger can be a powerful vehicle for justice and transformation:

▶ Kali is the energy we call upon to break off a dysfunctional relationship, or say hard things.

▶ Kali is the rage we embrace to uphold our boundaries and protect what is ours.

- ▶ Kali is the energy that says, "Stop being nice! Stand up for yourself!"
- ▶ Kali is the power that knows when death is the greatest form of kindness.

Although anger can be righteous, it must be managed responsibly so that its blaze is cleansing rather than destructive. Our anger is a sign that something needs to change; it is not a justification for bad behavior. Powerful feelings need to be processed and examined so that we can take action from our highest values. Conscious and accountable anger can provide the energy we need to make positive change. Wildfires are sometimes necessary to burn away the underbrush and make way for new growth.

"Bitterness is like cancer. It eats upon the host. But anger is like fire. It burns it all clean."

—Maya Angelou

REFLECTION

▶ What is your relationship to your own anger (consider that emotions such as irritation and frustration are forms of anger)?

▶ Recall a time that you were angry. What was your anger protecting or upholding?

▶ What kind of self-reflection process would help you listen to your anger and use it in service of good?

▶ Observe as feelings of irritation, frustration, and anger arise. What are these feelings protecting? When you examine your feelings, would giving voice to your anger support your highest values or is your anger pointing to something you personally need to work on and process?

▶ Is there anything in your life you need to end?

39. PLAY

Lila, Iccha-Skakti

In the beginning, there was Brahman (universal consciousness). Brahman was all that there was. Except for one other creature.

Lila approached Brahman and asked, rather mischievously, "Do you want to play a game?"

Brahman perked up. Why yes, he did.

"Okay," said Lila, "Go ahead and create the entire cosmos. Planets, stars, creatures…everything."

Brahman went into action and did as she suggested. He created the entire cosmos: planets, stars, and creatures.

"Alright," said Lila, "Great! Now cut yourself up into little pieces and put a little bit of yourself into everything that you have created."

Brahman looked at her doubtfully.

"Trust me, this is going to be great," Lila assured him.

So, Brahman, cut himself up into all the little pieces, and he put a little bit of himself — universal consciousness — into every single thing.

"Wonderful!" exclaimed Lila, clapping her hands. "Now...go find yourself!"

In tantric philosophy, *lila* means, "divine play," which describes the ultimate game of the universe. According to tantra, the great singularity of the shiva-shakti (universal consciousness and the energy of manifestation) chose to limit its own power so that it could experience manifestation (the physical world) in all its diversity of forms.

Another way to think of this: consider the big bang. Before the big bang, everything in the universe was encapsulated in a pure point of energy-matter-consciousness (according to yogis, this is shiva-shakti). As soon as the big bang occurred, the universe expanded and began to cool. It became limited in its own power, subject to laws of gravity, time, and physics. Only as the universe cooled could the myriad potential forms within that original singularity be expressed. Stars, planets, and life appeared.

From this perspective, the universe is the fabric of universal consciousness *(shiva)*, expressing itself in the manifest universe *(shakti)* through lila to experience the multiplicity in all its forms. One of those forms is you.

This is related to a concept called *iccha-shakti*, which is the divine creative urge for self-expression. Everything in the universe is in a state of expressing itself and its nature. Because we are a part of the universe, we can participate in this dance by consciously choosing to engage in joy and self-expression, simply for the joy of being who we really are.

REFLECTION

- ▶ What is your relationship to play?
- ▶ What is the benefit of play?
- ▶ Where can you cultivate more play and expression in your life?

40. EMBRACING EXPANSION AND CONTRACTION

Spanda

The universe is an expression of divine vibration, called *spanda*.

Everything is in a phase of expansion or contraction. Tides flow, the moon waxes and wanes, flowers bloom and die, we sleep and then we wake.

Both expansion and contraction are essential for life. While expansion facilitates growth, creativity, energy, and expression, contraction creates containment, stability, rest, and quietude. On a practical level, we cannot always be in expansion; we need rest and recovery in order to regain equilibrium.

As creatures of the universe, we are always participating in the flux of spanda. We experience it in a multiplicity of ways:

▶ Our lungs fill with air and then empty.

▶ Our heart fills with blood and then empties.

▶ We gain weight, we lose weight.

▶ We feel happy and expanded, then sad and contracted.

▶ Relationships feel close and intimate, then distant and disconnected.

- We long for connection, then we long to be alone.
- Abundance comes, then abundance goes.
- We give, and we receive.

All these fluctuations are part of the universal heartbeat.

When we are able to recognize that these fluctuations are the essential rhythm of the natural world, we can rest a little easier with the fluctuations that may come.

PRACTICE

- Come into a tall, comfortable seat.
- Take a few centering breaths.
- When your body feels calm and grounded, begin a counted pranayama practice: inhale for an internal count of four; exhale for an internal count of four.
- Repeat 5 to 10 times.
- Explore the feeling of expansion in your yoga practice.
- Focus on the inhalation.
- Stretch the body apart.
- Create space.

- ▶ What do you gain from expanding?
- ▶ Explore the feeling of contraction in your yoga practice.
- ▶ Focus on the exhalation.
- ▶ Pull the body together with muscular strength.
- ▶ Create stability.
- ▶ What do you gain from containment?

REFLECTION

- ▶ Do you have an easier time inhaling (receiving) or exhaling (giving)?
- ▶ How does the energy of expansion support you in life?
- ▶ How does the energy of contraction support you in life?

There is no need for temples; no need for complicated philosophy. Our own brain, our own heart is our temple; the philosophy is kindness.

—Dalai Lama

41. TRUE AND FALSE PERCEPTION

Pramana Vritti | Viparyaya Vritti

The Yoga tradition identifies a few different categories of "mind stuff" or "fluctuations" *(vritti)* to help us recognize and become friends with the workings of our minds.

The yogis were very clear that our perception of reality is limited to the information we can take in through our senses.

Consider these examples:

Although radio waves surround us, we lack the ability to perceive them without a radio.

Dogs can hear higher frequencies and smell far better than we can.

There are numerous wavelengths (infrared, gamma rays, X-rays) that we lack the ability to see.

The first viritti is true perception *(pramana viritti)*. True perception occurs when our idea of the world—that is, what we are experiencing and interpreting through our five senses—accurately matches reality. Although we can never be completely sure that we're correct, we are usually experiencing true perception if one of the following conditions is met:

- ▶ I perceive it directly. (I see a fire and know there is a fire.)

- ▶ Someone I trust has perceived it directly. (My best friend tells me that there is a fire.)

- ▶ There are enough clues that I can make a sensible inference based on my information. (I see smoke, hear fire trucks, and thus know that there is a fire.)

However, our human senses serve us very well, they are limited. And even when we do perceive the world directly, we can mistake our interpretations.

False perception *(viparyaya vritti)* occurs when we perceive the world directly, but interpret it in a way that doesn't align with how things really are.

Consider this traditional yoga story:

> A man is returning to his village at night. By the side of the road, he sees a giant and deadly snake. He runs to his village and warns everyone about the dangerous creature. When the villagers bring a lighted torch to see the snake, they discover that the snake was really just a coiled rope.

In this story, the man has directly perceived something, but his mind has misinterpreted the information. When the light is brought (representing illumination and knowledge), the villagers discover the truth.

We tend to accept our mind's interpretations as the truth. If I see my partner exuberantly embracing someone else, I may leap to conclusions about his fidelity before I find out that his long-lost cousin has come to town. Our minds filter our experiences through our expectations, needs, fears, wants, desires, and values.

We can often see this filtering process clearly in relationships, where we make conclusions about someone's actions based on our prior experiences. If I was hurt in a previous relationship because a partner cheated on me, I may interpret my new partner's actions through a veil of suspicion. If I am eager to make a new relationship work, I may overlook—or not even register—the red flags that keep cropping up.

Patanjali does not judge true perception as good and false perception as bad; he simply points out that our minds are constantly creating stories. By recognizing the nature of our minds, we can stay open to new information and not be so attached to our particular version of reality. We can create space and tolerance to question our assumptions, as well as have more compassion for other people who have different points of view.

As you begin to separate your stories from reality, you will be able to notice the filters (expectations, needs, wants, values, or fears) that are coloring your perception. Through this process, you can engage in a deep process of self-study *(svadhyaya)* and self-recognition. For example, when my partner looks irritated, my habitual reaction is to assume I've done something wrong. However, usually his frown has nothing to do with me and he's deep in thought. By noticing the story I create in my head, I can recognize how quick I am to leap to self-blame. Once I am aware of this conditioned response, I am better able to avoid distorting information in the future.

PRACTICE

▶ Come into a comfortable seat.

▶ Take a few deep, slow breaths.

▶ Slowly tune your attention to your sense of sight. Explore what you are really seeing. Can you see the space with "fresh eyes"? What is here that you've not seen before (or that you have filtered out)?

▶ Continue to explore your sense of sight, or you may cycle through your other senses (hearing, smell, touch, taste), allowing your mind the space and time to register the different kinds of information it can experience.

▶ After several minutes, reflect: on what was in reality that you had been filtering out?

▶ How does this change in perception shift your experience?

REFLECTION

▶ Consider a time that you misinterpreted reality. What did you perceive, and what did you assume? What led the misinterpretation?

▶ As you move through your day, slow down so that you may consider the information your senses are perceiving. See if you can catch yourself creating stories. (For example, my partner looks upset, and I interpret it to mean he is irritated with me.)

▶ Consider what expectations, needs, wants, desires, fears, or values are "coloring" your experience.

42. THE POWER OF IMAGINATION

Vikalpa vritti

The yogis were very clear that our perception of reality is limited to the information that we can take in through our five senses. When we perceive information and it accurately matches reality, it is called true perception. When we perceive information and it does not match reality, it is called false perception. And when we make up something in our minds that is not based in sensory perception, that is imagination *(vikalpa vritti)*.

It's human nature—and one of our gifts—to create stories and imagine new possibilities. Our ability to imagine new possibilities allows us to see a bird and fantasize about the possibility of flight. We taste peanut butter and chocolate and come up with a Reese's Peanut Butter Cup.

However, when left unchallenged, our imagination can take us down a dark path. When we don't recognize that our imagination is not reality, it can lead us to:

- ▶ Projection
- ▶ Unfounded expectations
- ▶ Missing present, real-world opportunities

- ▶ Unfounded fears
- ▶ Anxiety
- ▶ Delusion
- ▶ Paranoia

My dear friend was in a brief relationship in which she was constantly—and falsely—accused of infidelity. Sometimes her boyfriend would misinterpret events ("You're late! You were clearly out with someone else!") and sometimes he would just completely make up information ("You're thinking about someone else right now!").

Her partner wasn't a bad person, but his imagination was out of control. He wasn't able to see how his fabrications were distorting his perception of reality. Instead, he would be plagued with anxiety based on a deeper inner fear of abandonment and betrayal. Of course, the relationship couldn't withstand the stress of such unfounded fear for very long.

Because it can reveal our subconscious fears and desire, our imagination can provide us with potent and surprising personal insights. A daydream is like a little thought bubble sent up from our subconscious mind; when we're open to observing it, rather than simply believing or dismissing it, it can provide a window into our conditioning.

For example, after my divorce, I was not interested in starting a new relationship or being committed. Yet I would daydream about weddings! Even if I quickly dismissed these fantasies as absurd, the idea was coming from me. By recognizing the fantasy, I could acknowledge that a part of me wanted to marry again. Though our fantasies are certainly not reality, they can provide another avenue for self-study.

Recognizing the potency of imagination, we can also intentionally use it to create a positive experience. Affirmations and positive visualizations are powerful tools that leverage our imagination to support our lives.

PRACTICE

In the morning, pause and create a positive visualization for your day:

- ▶ Imagine yourself moving through your day with grace and lightness.
- ▶ Feel yourself how you wish to be as you interact with others.
- ▶ Imagine yourself moving through some of your daily activities with joy and ease.
- ▶ If you enjoy affirmations, repeat a positive affirmation to yourself deliberately several times to invite the energy of the affirmation into your life.

At the end of the day, consider how your visualization supported your experience.

REFLECTION:

▶ Are there any common themes to your daydreaming? What fears, needs, wants, desires, or values might they reveal?

▶ When has your imagination been an ally?

▶ When has your imagination been destructive?

▶ Throughout your day, notice when your mind begins to go into fantasy. What triggered vikalpa vritti? What did you get from it?

43. THE POWER OF MEMORY

Smriti Vritti

Memory operates on both a conscious and subconscious level. When we use our memory consciously, we delve into the rich storehouse of our past to gain information that is relevant to the present moment. For example, we might use memory to answer questions such as, When is my friend's birthday? or Where did I leave my keys?

Most of the time, however, our memory operates subconsciously to orient us in the present moment.

Imagine a car ride. The car is your physical body, your soul is the passenger, and the highway is the journey of your life. When you are born, your car is immaculate. The windows of your car are spotless and everything you can see out the windshield is clear and undistorted.

Then you begin your drive. You go everywhere. You drive through the dust of the desert, the pollen of spring flowers. Soon your new car is coated with a thick layer of dust: life has happened.

Now everything you perceive through the windshield is distorted by a thickening layer of grime from the road already traveled. Over time, you may even forget that there is a clear sight line to begin with, because now your world is seen entirely through the distortion of your smudgy, bug-covered windshield.

You see the present through the lens of the past.

As we begin to experience life—whether that experience is good, bad, sad, safe, scary, loving, or unhappy—we relate everything happening now to what has happened before. To keep us safe, our mind creates generalizations, infers meaning, and manufactures patterns.

It's important for human efficiency that this process is largely subconscious. (Just think about everything you would have to remember consciously to drive a car!) However, the subconscious nature of this process means that we will run on autopilot unless we check our assumptions.

On a very practical level, when I see a chair, I know it's a chair because I have learned that some sort of "chair-ness" exists in the world. Chairs have a seat, four legs, and are designed for humans to sit upon. In the world of relationships, I know I've met a good person because he or she acts in ways that I've previously perceived as "good."

Although memory provides us with the wisdom of experience, our previous conditioning makes it challenging for us to have a truly fresh experience. Derailing our assumptions can help us open to new possibilities.

REFLECTION:

▶ Explore what it is like to meet people in your life "freshly" and without expectations. If they were a strangers, how would your interaction change? This exploration can be particularly fun with someone with whom you have a long-standing relationship, like a partner or family member.

▶ Where in your life might memory be holding you back unnecessarily? Is there a way to mindfully check the waters again? As an example, I once took a bad fall out of a handstand, and so I believed for years that I couldn't do it. As it turns out, I was physically strong enough; I had to overcome the story in my mind to move forward.

▶ Consider a strong story from your past that feels negative. Can you rewrite that story now from a more compassionate and supportive point of view?

The Zen expression "Kill the Buddha!" means to kill any concept of the Buddha as something apart from oneself.

—Peter Matthiessen

44. EFFORT AND EASE

Asana

Only one sutra in *The Yoga Sutras* references physical posture. Though it most likely describes the qualities required to sit for meditation or pranayama, it also provides insight for how we can find a "seat" within ourselves.

Patanjali shares that there are two aspects to physical postures: steadiness and ease. A posture that is only steady *(sthira)* or only comfortable *(sukha)* is not asana. Instead, we must seek the balanced action of both strength and ease in our postures.

Most of us have an easier time with one aspect of the practice. Some of us are naturally adept at finding strength, stability, and intensity, although others will gravitate toward ease and letting go. Our yoga practice requires that we bring both of these qualities into balance.

This sutra is an invitation to consider how we balance effort and ease in all aspects of our lives.

....

"Asana is a steady, comfortable posture."
—Sutra 2.46

....

REFLECTION:

- What do I gain through ease?
- What do I gain through effort?
- Which do I tend to favor more instinctively?
- How can I cultivate practicing the opposite quality to invite balance into my life?
- Yoga practice: through the asana, mindfully invite the qualities for both sthira and sukha into each posture. (The exception: *savasana*; you are invited to completely let go in corpse pose.)

45. THE POWER OF BREATH

Pranayama

Life force *(prana)* is said to ride on the breath. By controlling the breath, we are able to harness this energy and consciously shift our energetic experience. Physiologically, controlling the breath enables us to indirectly access our nervous system. Though we can't consciously regulate our heart rate or blood pressure, we can indirectly access these systems through our breathing.

Interestingly, in Sanskrit, we cannot tell if the word *pranayama* is composed of *prana* and *yama* or *prana* and *ayama*. Pranayama can therefore mean both restraint and expansion of the breath and life force.

In *The Yoga Sutras*, Patanjali enumerates an eight-step process to yoga. Step four is pranayama. The yogis recognized that harnessing the breath is a potent and practical tool for managing the fluctuations of our minds.

PRACTICE

▶ Come into a comfortable seat.

▶ Take a few deep, expansive breaths, then allow your breath to return to its natural cadence.

▶ Sense the quality of your thoughts and your feelings.

▶ Maintaining the ease in your body, inhale for a count of four, then exhale for a count of four.

▶ If your breath is relaxed and without anxiety, you can extend the count (inhale for a count of five, exhale for a count of five, etc.).

▶ If your body can remain relaxed, begin to lengthen the slight pause between the inhale and exhale.

▶ After a few minutes, let the counting go and return to your natural breath.

▶ Again, sense the quality of your thoughts and your feelings.

▶ What has shifted?

REFLECTION

Pranayama can involve a dedicated seated breath practice, but it also includes being aware of your breath as you move through your daily life. As yogis, we can take responsibility for our inner state of energy by using the breath to support our self-regulation:

▶ Throughout your day, pause to notice the different qualities of your breathing (fast, slow, shallow, deep, chest/belly, rough, smooth). Become curious about how different breath qualities may reflect different emotional or mental states.

▶ Begin to incorporate the simple practice of taking three deep, conscious breaths throughout your day to find a personal "reset."

▶ Explore how you can use your breath to support your emotional and mental state:

   ▶ When you are agitated or anxious, practice slowing your breath or lengthening your exhale.

   ▶ When you feel tired, practice lengthening your exhale or taking a few deep sighs to move your energy.

▶ Explore breathing into different parts of your torso: the belly, side ribs, upper chest, upper back, lower back. If you find it hard to access the breath in part of your body, you can enhance your breath awareness by physically stretching that area. For example, if you find it challenging to access breath movement in your upper back, then come into a cat pose and "send" your breath between your shoulder blades.

Keep in mind: there is no one "right" way to breathe. Our body and breathing will naturally shift to accommodate what is needed in the moment. Jogging will require a faster and more rigorous breath pattern than lying in savasana. Our intention is to cultivate flexibility, resiliency, and mindfulness in our breath and our energy.

46. UNDERSTANDING THE SELF: ANXIETY

Vata

Tracing its roots back to the Vedas, Ayurveda an ancient and holistic healing art designed to promote health and longevity, and the sister science to yoga. Healing is achieved through looking at all areas of life: exercise, sleep, activities, massage, self-care practices, and nutrition.

According to Ayurveda and yogic philosophy, the material world consists of five great elements: earth, water, fire, air, ether. Each person's innate disposition *(prakruti)* is determined by how these elements are expressed in their constitution through their *doshas*.

Doshas are composed of two of the five elements. There are three doshas:

▶ Vata: composed of ether and air

▶ Pitta: composed of fire and water

▶ Kapha: composed of water and earth

Although we each are influenced by all three doshas, usually we have one dominant and one subdominant dosha that govern our nature.

Vata

The qualities of vata are similar to those of air and space: light, moving, mobile, quick, cool, dry, spacious, rough, irregular, quick, and changeable. Physically, vata governs digestion, the nervous system, and movement.

People with a balanced vata dosha will be creative, light, agile, charismatic, adventurous, and curious. People who are vata dominant are quick-witted and love excitement.

An excess of vata may be expressed in the following symptoms:

▶ Nervousness

▶ Spaciness

▶ Anxiety, worry

▶ Delusion

▶ Feeling hyped up, jittery

▶ Feeling cold

▶ Unable to sleep soundly

▶ Flatulent (too much wind)

▶ Constipated (too dry)

▶ Dry skin

REFLECTION:

If you are suffering from too much vata, consider implementing some of the following self-care strategies to counterbalance the energy of this dosha:

► Engage in warm, slow practices such as hot yin, restorative or hatha yoga.

► Eat warm, grounding foods (roasted root vegetables, soups.

► Enjoy a warming sauna.

► Sit on the earth (grounding).

► Meditate on connecting to the earth.

► Avoid stimulants like caffeine.

► Slow down (breathe slowly, lie down, or take 10 deep, slow breaths).

► Go to bed early.

► Lie down with sandbags or blankets on you (grounding).

► Avoid stimulation, enjoy a retreat from distractions and busyness.

► Enjoy an oil massage.

► Avoid stressful situations.

47. UNDERSTANDING THE SELF: ANGER AND CONTROL

Pitta

The qualities of a pitta-dominant personality are similar to those of fire and water (think of a fluidlike oil): fiery, fierce, bright, smart, leading, "type A," energetic, directive. Physically, pitta governs digestion (the energy of fire and transformation).

When pitta is excessive, it may be expressed in the following symptoms:

▶ Domination

▶ Impatience

▶ Punitive behavior

▶ Overly controlling actions

▶ Anger

▶ Acne (too oily, inflamed)

▶ Inflammation/rashes

▶ Ulcers, heartburn (too much acid, heat)

REFLECTION

If you are suffering from too much pitta, consider implementing some of the following self-care strategies to counterbalance the energy of this dosha:

▶ Engage in cooling practices such as flow, yin, restorative or hatha yoga.

▶ Eat cooling foods (cucumbers, melons, fruit).

▶ Rest.

▶ Avoid stress and take a break.

▶ Take cool baths.

▶ Eat regularly.

▶ Enjoy cooling scents or oils (lavender, jasmine, mint).

▶ Focus on pacifying pranayama or meditation practices.

48. UNDERSTANDING THE SELF: LETHARGY AND DEPRESSION

Kapha

The qualities of a kapha-dominant personality are similar to those of earth and water: stable, grounded, rooted, connected, strong, sturdy, thoughtful, compassionate, loyal, and patient.

When kapha is excessive, it may be expressed in the following symptoms:

- Lethargy
- Heaviness
- Slowness
- Weight gain
- Depression
- Stubbornness
- Intractability
- Lack of flow
- Hoarding

REFLECTION:

If you are suffering from too much kapha, consider implementing some of the following self-care strategies to counterbalance the energy of this dosha:

▶ Energize with practices such as power and flow yoga.

▶ Seek out stimulation and excitement.

▶ Get out of the house and into the world.

▶ Eat lightly; enjoy lighter foods and season your food with spice.

▶ Clear your space of clutter and stuff.

▶ Get moving by going for walks or practicing light cardio.

▶ Enjoy warm, stimulating scents like rosemary, eucalyptus or peppermint.

▶ Avoid sweet and heavy foods.

▶ Engage in kriya yoga practices like kapalabhati.

49. SPEECH

Mauna

Speech is powerful.

In Hinduism, Sanskrit is understood to be a divine language. The words do not only represent objects; the sounds themselves are believed to contain the divine essence of the object they describe. Many traditions recognize speech as a creative power; the Old Testament begins, "In the beginning was the Word ... and the Word was God."

Speech creates meaning. When we speak, we become creators with the capacity to both uplift as well as destroy. Consider the damaging power of gossip: once a rumor has been started, it's impossible to fully erase the story from our minds, even if it's untrue. In our modern world, our "speech" can include all the ways we may use words: emails, texts, and posts on social media.

We often forget about the power of our words and may use them carelessly.

Taking time to examine our relationship to speech can help us to become more mindful in our expression and be present in this moment. The practice of silence *(mauna)* can help us recognize the enormous amount of energy output that speaking requires. When we restrain our speech, we become aware of the impact our words can have. Practicing silence helps our minds to become calmer; we become more interested in taking in the world, rather than filling it.

PRACTICE

▶ Choose a time where you will be able to practice silence for at least a few hours, or even a day.

▶ Reflect on what practicing silence give you.

REFLECTION

▶ What is the quality of your speech?

▶ Why do you speak?

▶ Do you use speech to cover up discomfort (filling the silence, avoiding real communication or vulnerability)?

▶ Do you ever speak when you're not sure if someone else is interested?

▶ Practice being "impeccable with your word" (*The Four Agreements*, don Miguel Ruiz) and speaking only with integrity (*satya*) for one day. What is the result?

50. RITUALS

Vedas

Many cultures have used rituals to generate power, commune with natural and supernatural forces, and achieve transcendental states of insight. The rituals of Vedic culture (ancient Hinduism) included fire rituals, sacrificial rituals, and use of plant medicine.

A modern yoga practice has its own set of rituals: placing the mat to create a sacred space, becoming conscious of the breath and body, engaging in focus and discipline during the practice, death meditation *(savasana)*, and then the return to the world.

However, beyond our yoga practice, creating a personal ritual can support us in creating a framework of mindfulness for our day. We can use a ritual to set an intention, connect with our highest self, and steer our own course.

REFLECTION

Create a ritual that you can do each morning or each evening. Your ritual doesn't have to be long; even five minutes can help you create a mindful state.

Consider what you wish to create in your ritual. What activities or contemplations will help you reconnect to your self and your values?

Your ritual might include the following:

▶ Write or journal.

▶ List what you are grateful for.

▶ Do a brief asana practice to connect with your body.

▶ Consciously breathe or meditate.

▶ Set a written/spoken intention.

▶ Read an inspirational quote.

▶ Listen to inspirational or elevating music.

51. TAKING SPACE FROM THE WORLD

Pratyahara

Have you ever wished to just get away from it all?

The world is full of distractions, obligations, and stress. When we get pulled in every direction it's easy to lose our sense of groundedness, stability, and ease. Nourishing our introspective capacity is a vital act of self-care.

In *The Yoga Sutras*, Patanjali enumerates an eight-step process to yoga. Step five is *pratyahara*, or sense withdrawal. Part of the journey toward meditation and personal insight is to take a retreat from the distractions of the world.

In meditation, pranayama, or asana practice, this withdrawal effortlessly occurs as we become less interested in the outer world. You may have experienced this on your mat as your mind naturally becomes quieter and less restless during your practice.

Our senses—and our minds—are habituated to racing after what brings us pleasure, like coffee, chocolate, praise, or material acquisitions. When we become grounded in ourselves (sometimes just by taking 10 slow, conscious breaths), the clamoring of these compulsions begins to quiet. As the senses withdraw, we become less compulsive and attracted to objects in the outer world. As our inner sense of self begins to stabilize, we reconnect to our fundamental ground of being and presence.

REFLECTION

How can you support taking a personal retreat from the world?

Consider the following:

▶ Enjoy a daily meditation. Even two minutes can be nourishing.

▶ Withdraw from technology: turn off computers and phones for a designated length of time.

▶ Take time in nature.

▶ Take a weekend retreat.

▶ Embrace a daily "quiet time" practice.

▶ Give yourself permission to be unavailable to others.

▶ Create daily, uninterrupted, "self" time.

52. COMMUNITY

Kula

Your *kula* is your community, clan, or family. In yoga, a kula is your spiritual community, which comes together with a shared intention and purpose for growth and connection. Within our kula, we find a trustworthy support network to wrestle with spiritual questions and support one another through the challenges of daily life.

The yoga path can sometimes look solitary. After all, one chapter of *The Yoga Sutras* is entitled "Aloneness"! Kula reminds us that although our yoga path is often introspective and personal, we can choose to travel our path in very good company. When we connect to—or create—a community of like-minded souls, we have the opportunity to give and receive support for our highest intentions, and support one another in upholding our most precious values.

Seeking support on this path is a sign of wisdom.

REFLECTION

▶ Who do you consider part of your kula?

▶ Do you have new relationships you wish to nourish?

▶ What further communities/resources could support your path?

▶ How can you set time aside to nourish your heart connections?

CONCLUSION

"The nature of practice
is continual, devoted,
and for a long time."

—Sutra 1.14

Now that you have begun to use some of these concepts and tools, continue to explore how they can guide and support your work, play, and relationships. And be patient: yoga is a practice for a lifetime (or, according to the yogis, several lifetimes!) and we will often need to learn its lessons again and again.

Living our yoga is an invitation to stay awake, aware, and curious. When our minds create stories or we feel reactive, yoga asks us to perk up and lean in. Rather than live on autopilot, we can do our best to stay open to the freshness of this moment. Through this practice, we can start to experience the world as it is, rather than living through the lens of our assumptions and expectations.

POSES

Corpse Pose, page 203

Cat/Cow Pose, page 204

Easy Seat, page 205

Skull-Shining Breath, page 206

Satisfying Hip Opening, pages 207–208

Happy Heart Opener, pages 209–212

Child's Pose, page 213

90/90 Pose, page 214

Low Lunge, page 214–215

Pigeon Pose, page 215

Eye of the Needle Pose, page 216

Mountain Pose, pages 216–217

Downward-Facing Dog, page 217

Halfway Lift, page 218

High-Crescent Lunge, page 218–219

Forward Fold, page 219

Hero's Pose, page 220

CORPSE POSE

(Savasana)

▶ Lie prone on your back with legs extended. Turn your palms up and lay them a few inches from your sides or on your chest and stomach. Let your body fully relax. Close your eyes. Take several long, smooth breaths and release the tension from your body. Let your breathing slow down. Remain in this pose for a least 5 minutes.

▶ To come out, draw your knees into your chest and roll onto your right side. Cradle your head on your right arm and take a few breaths. When you're ready to sit, use your top hand to press yourself slowly to a comfortable seat. Take a few slow breaths.

CAT/COW POSE

(Marjaryasana/Bitilasana)

▸ Begin on your hands and knees. Place your palms under your shoulders and set your knees under your hips. As you inhale, drop your belly toward the earth, reach your chest forward through your arms, and tip your lower back up to the sky.

▸ As you exhale, press through your hands, look toward your belly, and round your spine upward. Continue arching and rounding your spine to find length through the front and back of your body. Link your breathing with the movement, feeling your body open on the inhale, and contract on the exhale.

EASY SEAT

(Sukhasana)

▶ Sit cross-legged, crossing at your shins. Switch legs so that your "non-traditional" shin is in front. Your shins should be placed far enough away that there is an open, triangular space between your hips and legs. Relax your legs fully. Rock slightly to find the center of your tailbone. Stretch your spine. Place your hands on your thighs and draw your arms back. Inhale and allow your ribs to expand. As you exhale, feel the subtle lifting of your pelvic floor. Soften your muscles, your face, and your eyes. Keeping the back of your neck long, tip your chin toward your chest until you feel a soft tension through the front of your throat, as if you were holding an orange beneath your chin. Your body is now ready to meditate.

SKULL-SHINING BREATH

(Kapalabhati)

▶ To begin, sit either on the floor, on a block, or on the edge of a chair. Lift tall through your spine and reach your arms overhead in a wide V position. Take a deep inhale, then exhale fully. Inhale halfway, then begin a series of short, sharp exhales through your nose at a rate of about 1 to 2 per second. Allow your inhales to drop in naturally and keep your chest lifted and open. Exhale 25 times. Take a few natural breaths in and out to conclude the pose.

SATISFYING HIP OPENING

▶ Begin in **Child's Pose** (see page 213) with your knees out wide and take 10 deep breaths. Allow your pelvis to get heavier against your heels and deliberately release your body weight downward. Relax your shoulders, arms, and torso.

▶ Come onto all fours and take 5 to 10 rounds of **Cat/Cow Pose** (see page 204) to release any tension through your spine. Feel free to roll your shoulders and shift your hips from side to side. Step your right foot forward into **Low Lunge** (see page 214). If you are able, you can allow your knee to move in front of your ankle to stretch through your calf. Be careful of overextending your knee. Keep your hands on your front thigh, or reach your arms up to the sky to stretch the side of your waist. Squeeze your right glute to stretch the front of your hip. Take 5 deep breaths, then change sides.

▶ Sit on your right hip and bring your right shin parallel with the short end of your mat. Place your left shin parallel to the long edge of your mat similar to the **90/90 Pose** (see page 214) and inhale. As you exhale, hinge over your front thigh to stretch your outer hip. For this variation on **Pigeon Pose** (see page 214), keep your right hip anchored to the earth and slide your left leg back behind you until you feel a deep stretch through your outer right hip. Stay for 10 to 15 breaths. You can switch out **Pigeon Pose** with **Eye of the Needle Pose** (see page 216), depending on your comfort level.

HAPPY HEART OPENER

▶ Start in **Mountain Pose** (see page 216) and take 3 deep breaths. Reach your arms up overhead, turn your right palm upward, and hold onto your right wrist with your left hand. Relax your shoulders and press your tailbone downward. Lean into your right foot and curve your left side up and over to the left into an arch, bending at the waist. To deepen this side stretch, lift your left foot. Hold for 3 breaths, then change sides.

► Inhale and reach your arms up, then exhale into **Forward Fold** (see page 219). Inhale to come into **Halfway Lift** (see page 218), then exhale and step your left foot back. Rise up into **High-Crescent Lunge** (see page 218). Interlace your hands behind your head and point your elbows forward to relax your shoulders outward.

▶ Balance back onto your legs, keeping your weight centered over them. Press your chest back, tense your left glute, and straighten your back leg. Press your head into your hands and reach your chest forward and up. Take a deep breath. Lean into the ball of your back foot and push your front heel down to lift your stomach up. Tense your core as you exhale, then inhale to reach your arms straight upward. On your next exhale, press into your feet and bring your hands to the floor. Step forward, come into **Forward Fold**, and take 3 breaths. Step your right foot back and repeat **High-Crescent Lunge** on the opposite side.

▶ As you step to the front of your mat, inhale and come into **Halfway Lift**. Bring your hands to your hips, then inhale and stand up. Place your hands on your heart in **Mountain Pose** and hold as long as feels nourishing.

CHILD'S POSE

(Balasana)

▶ Sit with your toes together and your knees a little wider than hip distance apart.

▶ Hinge forward from your hips to place your forehead on the earth or a block. Allow your arms to fall where feels comfortable. Check the position of your forehead against the floor and ensure that the skin of your forehead is wrinkling down toward the bridge of your nose rather than up. Let your face relax. Allow your head to get heavy and your belly to be soft and open. As you inhale, feel your breath move into your back ribs and lower back. As you exhale, allow any muscular tension to soften and let go. Remain in the pose for as long as feels nourishing. Then you come out, take a few moments to stretch the backs of your knees by extending your legs back, or come into **Downward-Facing Dog** (see page 217).

90/90 POSE

▶ From a seated position on your mat, place your right leg directly in front of you with your knee flat on the ground. Be sure to keep your leg at a right angle. Repeat this motion with your left leg, moving it behind you.

▶ Slowly bring your chest down toward your knee, keeping your shoulders squared and remembering to breathe. Keep your elbows close to your body unless they can reach your mat evenly, then rest them on your mat. Hold for 20 to 60 seconds, or lean further forward to intensify the stretch, completing 6 to 10 repetitions of 3 seconds each.

LOW LUNGE
(Anjaneyasana)

▶ Begin on all fours with your hands just wider than your shoulders and your knees just behind your hips. Place your right foot by your right thumb. Bring your hands to your right thigh to lift your torso upward. Square your hips with your tailbone pointing down. Settle your hips forward and down to stretch the front of your left thigh. Be sure to keep your knee over your right heel.

- Draw your front ribs in and reach your arms forward and up in a wide V. Press your thighs together for stability. Draw your chest out into a mini backbend. Stretch through the length of your torso and out through your fingertips. Take 3 deep breaths. You can choose to keep your left knee down or lifted. As you exhale, bring your hands to your front thigh and then your mat. Step your right foot back, take a few breaths in **Child's Pose** (see page 213), and repeat on the other side.

PIGEON POSE
(Eka Pada Kapotasana)

- Beginning on hands and knees, bring your right knee to rest on the floor behind your right hand. Angle your right foot toward the left side of your mat, stretching your hip and not your knee. Flex your foot to stabilize the pose.

- Slowly extend your left leg straight back until it rests on the floor. Lift your pelvis, squaring it to your mat. If your right hip raises, rest on a blanket or block. Exhale and slowly walk your hands forward. Bring your torso to rest on the floor, or rest on your elbows. Hold for 5 breaths. Walk your hands back to rest slightly wider than shoulder width. Lift your collarbones and inhale to return upright. Hold for 5 breaths, then move into **Child's Pose** (see page 213).

EYE OF THE NEEDLE POSE
(*Sucirandhrasana*)

▶ Begin in **Hero's Pose** (see page 220), then recline onto your back. Cross your right ankle over your left knee and draw your left knee into your chest, keeping the back of your shin against your thigh. Breathe into the tightness of your outer hip and allow your right hip to settle toward your body. Close your eyes and let your head rest onto the floor. Take 10 deep breaths, then slowly change sides.

MOUNTAIN POSE
(*Tadasana*)

▶ Stand with your feet either hip distance apart or together and parallel to each other. Lift your toes and stretch your inner and outer arches. Keeping your arches lightly stretched, relax your toes and press your feet downward. Engage the top of your thighs, with your tailbone pointing down and pelvis even. Draw your lower belly slightly in and up, then inhale and lengthen your waist. Roll your shoulders back and down and stretch your fingertips downward. Relax your front ribs in and down and draw your shoulder blades slightly together. Stretch your neck so your chin is level with the floor. Relax your eyes and take 5 to 10 deep breaths, becoming aware of the strength of your body.

DOWNWARD-FACING DOG
(Adho Mukha Svanasana)

▶ Begin on hands and knees. Turn your hands so your index fingers point forward and spread your fingers wide. Press into your fingers to take weight off of your wrists. Curl your toes under and lift your knees slightly.

▶ Keeping your knees bent, send your hips toward the sky. Press your index knuckles down and your forearms toward each other, then press your upper arms upward to relax your neck. Keeping your spine long, straighten your legs. Stretch from your hands through to your heels. Take 5 to 10 deep breaths. On your last exhale, slowly lower your knees and sit your hips back on your heels to come into **Child's Pose** (see page 213).

HALFWAY LIFT
(Ardha Uttanasana)

▶ Begin in **Forward Fold** (see page 25). Place your hands on either your shins or the floor in front of your feet. Inhale, straighten your arms, and unfold your torso outward as far as you can, creating a space between your pelvis and navel.

▶ Pushing down with your hands, lift your sternum up and forward. Bend your knees as you arch your back, allowing the stretch to move through your shoulders and over the curve of your back down to your waist. Keeping your eyes forward and your neck long, hold the position for a few breaths. Exhale and return to **Forward Fold**.

HIGH-CRESCENT LUNGE

▶ Begin in **Downward-Facing Dog** (see page 217) and raise your right leg toward the sky.

- Step your right foot to your right thumb, keeping your feet hip distance apart. Place your hand on your front thigh and lift your torso up to come into a high lunge. Lengthen your tailbone downward and straighten your back leg, keeping your left heel lifted. Reach your arms up by your ears into a wide Y shape. Lift your chest forward and up for a gentle backbend. Hold for 5 deep breaths and feel your inner body expand and open. On your final exhale, slowly bring your hands to the floor, step into **Downward-Facing Dog**, and take a few breaths before repeating on the other side.

FORWARD FOLD
(Uttanasana)

- Stand with your feet hip distance apart and parallel. Inhale, roll your shoulders back, and lift your chest to lengthen your spine.

- As you exhale, bend your knees and hinge forward from your hips. If possible, bring your chest onto your thighs so that your upper body is supported by your legs. Fold forward as deeply as you can with a straight spine, allow your back to round, and release your head toward the earth. Take a few deep breaths, feeling the backs of your legs open and releasing any tension through your neck and jaw. Let your upper body hang heavy. To come out, relax your knees, bring your hands to your hips, and lift your shoulders. Press through your feet and slowly rise to stand.

HERO'S POSE

(Virasana)

▶ Stack one or two blocks on top of each other. Sit on the blocks so that your ankles hug the outside of the blocks and your thighs are close and parallel to each other. Adjust your sitting height as needed for comfort. Rock slightly to find the center of your tailbone. Place your hands on your upper thighs, with palms facing up or down. Draw your arms back to widen your collarbones. Inhale and feel your lungs and ribs expand. As you exhale, feel the subtle lifting of your pelvic floor. Soften your muscles, your face, and your eyes. Keeping the back of your neck long, tip your chin toward your chest until you feel a soft tension through the front of your throat, as if you were holding an orange beneath your chin.

FURTHER READING:

Light on Life, B. K. S. Iyengar

The Deeper Dimensions of Yoga, Theory and Practice, Georg Feuerstein

The Heart of Yoga, T. K. V. Desikachar

The Power of Now, Eckhart Tolle

Eastern Body, Western Mind, Anodea Judith

When Things Fall Apart, Pema Chodron

The Yoga Sutras of Patanjali (translations by Chip Hartranft and Swami Satchidananda are used in this book)

INDEX

abhinivesa (fear of death), 128–129

abhyasa (practice), 86

absolute, connecting to the, 41–44

ahamkara (ego), 106–107, 110

ahimsa (nonviolence), 85–87, 90

ajna chakra, 143–144

alchemy, transformation and, 147–148

anahata (heart) *chakra*, 139–140

anava mala, 99–101

Angelou, Maya, 150

anger, 149–151, 183–184

anxiety, 180–182

aparigraha (non-grasping), 96–98

Arjuna, 22, 35, 77–79

asana, 174–175

ashtanga yoga, 85

asteya (non-stealing), 96–98

avidya (non-seeing), 32, 97, 120–122

Ayurveda, 180

baggage, letting go of, 34–37

Bhagavad Gita, 20–21, 22–23, 35, 36, 61, 77–79, 81

bhakti yoga (yoga of devotion), 22, 62, 81–84

big bang, 153

"Blind Men and the Elephant, The," 16–17

body-based meditation, 70

body-centered practices, 20

brahmacharya (abstinence), 68–71

breath, power of, 176–179

buddhi (higher mind), 107, 110

Buddhism, 17

Carvaka, 17

Cat/Cow Pose, 204

celibacy, 68, 73

chakras, 133–146

change, fear of, 128–132

changing negative thoughts, 45–48

Chariot Story, 72

Child's Pose, 213

Chodron, Pema, 37

Clark, Gene, 108

communication, 141–142

community, 193–194

comparison and jealousy, 102–105

compassion, 52–54, 85–87

conflict, 77–80, 123–124

connecting to the absolute, 41–44

connection and love, 81–84

contentment, 117–119

contraction, embracing expansion and, 155–157

control, anger and, 183–184

Corpse Pose, 203

cultivating fire, 137–138

cultivating flow, 135–136

cultivating stability, 133–134

Dalai Lama, 158

darshanas (viewpoints), 16

dharma (duty), 22, 61–63

dhyaya (contemplate), 123

disconnection, sadness and, 99–101

dislike, 126–127

doshas, 180–186

Downward-Facing Dog, 217

dualist philosophy, 21–22

dvesha (aversion), 126–127

earth energy, 133–134

ease, effort and, 174–175

Easy Seat, 205

effort and ease, 174–175

Einstein, Albert, 103

expansion and contraction, embracing, 155–157

Eye of the Needle Pose, 216

false identities, letting go of, 38–40

false perception, true and, 160–164

fear of change, 128–132

filters, 161–162

fire

    cultivating, 137–138

    for transformation, 66–67

fire energy, 137–138

five acts, 94–95

flow, cultivating, 135–136

for surrender, 111–113

Forward Fold, 219

Frankl, Viktor E., 62

Gandhi, Mahatma, 64, 131

giving and receiving love, 139–140

grasping, 96–98

great mistake, 31, 50, 97

gunas (forces of nature), 69

gurus, 19

habits, changing, 35

Halfway Lift, 218

happiness and suffering, 120–122

Happy Heart Opener, 209–212

happy people, how to relate to, 49–51

Hartranft, Chip, 85

hatha yoga, 20, 70, 147–148

Heart of Recognition, The (Kshema-raja), 94
Hedley, Gil, 74
High-Crescent Lunge, 218–219
Hinduism, 15–18
householders, 20
how to relate to happy people, 49–51
how to relate to sad people, 52–54
how to relate to virtuous people, 55–57
how to relate to wicked people, 58–60

iccha-shakti, 153
imagination, power of, 165–168
Indian culture, 15–16
Indus Valley Civilization, 18
inner critic, 45–48
intensity, 66–67
internal conflict, 56–57
Isvara (pure awareness), 41
isvara pranidhana (yoga of action), 111–113
Iyengar, B.K.S., 73

Jainism, 17
jealousy, comparison and, 102–105
jnana (wisdom), 21
jnana yoga (yoga of wisdom), 22, 77–80

Kali, 149–151
kapha, 180, 185–186
karma (residue of cause and effect), 19, 35–36
karma yoga (yoga of action), 22, 34–37
Katha Upanishad, 72
Krishna, 22, 35–36, 78, 81
kriya yoga (yoga of action), 111–112, 123
Kshemaraja, Rajanaka, 94
kula (community), 193–194

lethargy and depression, 185–186
letting go of baggage, 34–37
letting go of false identities, 38–40
lila (divine play), 152–154
love
    bhakti yoga (yoga of devotion) and, 81–84
    connection and, 81–84
    giving and receiving, 139–140
Low Lunge, 214–215
lying, 90–93

Mahabharata, The ("Great War"), 22, 35
mahabhutas (elements), 69
manas (mind), 73, 106
manipura chakra, 137–138
manomaya kosha (mind layer), 73
Matthiessen, Peter, 172
mauna (silence), 187–188
mayiya mala, 102–105
meditation, 11, 19
memory, power of, 169–171
Mimamsa (interpretation of the Vedas), 17
mind, human, 29–33, 45–48, 106–110
Mountain Pose, 216–217
muladhara (root) *chakra*, 133–134

negative thoughts, changing, 45–48
neti, neti (not this, not this), 37–39
90/90 Pose, 214
nonviolence, 85–87
Nyaya (logic), 17

om, 41–44

Patanjali. See *Yoga Sutras of Patanjali, The*
perception, true and false, 160–164

Pigeon Pose, 215
pitta, 180, 183–184
play, 152–154
pleasure, 72–76
poses, 203–219
power of breath, 176–179
power of imagination, 165–168
power of memory, 169–171
prakriti (physical world), 68–69
pramana vritti (true perception), 160–164
prana (energy), 19, 176
pranayama, 176–179
pratipaksha bhavanam, 45–48
pratyahara (sense withdrawal), 191–192
purification, 114–116
purusha (witness; true self), 30–31, 45, 50, 69

questions
    Who am I? 29–33
    Why am I here? 61–63
    Why is my mind so crazy? 106–110
    why we forget, 94–95

raga (pleasure), 72–76
receiving love, giving and, 139–140
ritualistic chants, 18
rituals, 189–190
Rumi, 16

sad people, how to relate to, 52–54
sadness and disconnection, 99–101
sahasrara (crown chakra), 145–146
samhara (reabsorption), 94
Samkhya, 17
samsara (suffering), 35
samskara (impression), 34–35
santosha, 117–119

Satchidananda, Swami, 58, 111
satya (truthfulness), 90–93
sauca (purification), 114–116
self, sense of, 29–33
self-blame, 118
self-expression, 141–142, 153
self-study, 111, 123–125, 162
sense organs, 106
sense withdrawal (*pratyahara*), 191
sexuality, 68–71, 135–136
Shakespeare, William, 30
shakti, 69, 153
Sharma, Robin, 106
shiva, 69, 153
Skull-Shining Breath, 206
smriti vritti, 169–171
smrti, 107
spanda (divine vibration), 155–157
speech, 187–188
spiritual liberation, 124
spirituality, 145–146
srsti (act of creation), 94
stability, cultivating, 133–134
steadiness, 174
sthira (steady), 174
sthiti (stasis), 94
stickiness, 96–98
suffering, happiness and, 120–122
sukha (comfortable), 174
surrender, for, 111–113
Suzuki, D. T., 24
sva (self), 123
svadhisthana (sweetness) *chakra*, 135–136
svadhyaya (self-study), 111, 123–125, 162

taking space from the world, 191–192
tantric philosophy/yoga, 20, 68–70, 74,

99, 102, 147, 153
tapas, 66–67, 111
tat tvam asi, 61
third eye, 143–144
thought(s), 29–33, 45–48, 145–146
timers, 11
tips for practices, 11
tirodhana (concealment), 94–95
Tolle, Eckhart, 89
transformation and alchemy, 147–148
true and false perception, 160–164
truthfulness, 90–93

understanding the self
    anger and control, 183–184
    anxiety, 180–182
    lethargy and depression, 185–186
universal consciousness, 68–69
Upanishads, 18–19

Vaisheshika (atomism), 17
vata, 180–182
Vedanta ("end" of the Vedas), 17
Vedas, 17, 18, 19, 189–190
vikalpa vritti (imagination), 165–168
viparyaya vritti (false perception), 160–164
virtuous people, how to relate to, 55–57
vishuddha (throat) *chakra*, 141–142
vision, 143–144
viveka (discrimination), 107
vrittis (fluctuations of mind and memory), 107

water energy, 135–136
Who am I? 29–33
Why am I here? 61–63

Why is my mind so crazy? 106–110
why we forget, 94–95
wicked people, how to relate to, 58–60
world, taking space from the, 191–192
worldly renunciation, 20
world-positive viewpoint, 20

Yamada, Koun, 43
yamas (external disciplines), 85–86, 90
yoga
    benefits of, 9
    history of, 15–23
Yoga Sutras of Patanjali, The
    about, 19–22
    on aloneness, 193
    on ashtanga yoga, 85
    on *avidya*, 120
    on Isvara, 41
    on kriya yoga, 111
    on negative thoughts, 45
    on physical posture, 174
    on pleasure, 72–73
    on practice, 198
    on *pranayama*, 176
    on *pratyahara*, 191
    on relating to others, 52, 55, 58–59
    on relating to the world, 97
    on who we are, 31
    on *yamas*, 90
yogas chitta vritti nirodhah, 29–33

zen, 24, 43, 108

ABOUT CIDER MILL PRESS BOOK PUBLISHERS

Good ideas ripen with time. From seed to harvest, Cider Mill Press brings fine reading, information, and entertainment together between the covers of its creatively crafted books. Our Cider Mill bears fruit twice a year, publishing a new crop of titles each spring and fall.

"Where Good Books Are Ready for Press"

Visit us on the web at
www.cidermillpress.com
or write to us at
PO Box 454
12 Spring St.
Kennebunkport, Maine 04046